Guided Inquiry

Learning in the 21st Century

Carol C. Kuhlthau,
Leslie K. Maniotes, and
Ann K. Caspari

LIBRARIES
UNLIMITED
A Member of the Greenwood Publishing Group

Westport, Connecticut • London

Library of Congress Cataloging-in-Publication Data

Kuhlthau, Carol Collier, 1937-
  Guided inquiry : learning in the 21st century school / Carol C. Kuhlthau, Leslie K. Maniotes, and Ann K. Caspari.
    p. cm.
  Includes bibliographical references and index.
  ISBN-13: 978–1–59158–435–3 (alk. paper)
  1. Learning. 2. Motivation in education. 3. Information literacy—Study and teaching (Higher) 4. Information technology. I. Maniotes, Leslie K., 1967– II. Caspari, Ann K., 1965– III. Title.
  LB1060.K84 2007
  371.39—dc22   2007017725

British Library Cataloguing in Publication Data is available.

Library of Congress Catalog Card Number: 2007017725
ISBN-13: 978-1-59158-435-3

First published in 2007

Libraries Unlimited, Inc., 88 Post Road West, Westport, CT 06881
A Member of the Greenwood Publishing Group, Inc.
www.lu.com

Printed in the United States of America

∞

The paper used in this book complies with the Permanent Paper Standard issued by the National Information Standards Organization (Z39.48-1984).

10 9 8 7 6 5 4 3 2 1

This book is dedicated to Lily, Charlie, Elizabeth, Owen, Jack, Emma, and all students of the 21st century.

Contents

List of Illustrations

Preface

Guided Inquiry has its foundation in my research and writings on the student's perspective of the constructive process of learning from a variety of sources. The development of this program grew from three previously published books. *School Librarian's Grade by Grade Activities Program* (1981) presented a sequential library skills program to match the developmental stages and specific library and information needs of students at each grade level, kindergarten through eighth grade. *Teaching the Library Research Process* (1985; 2nd ed. 1994) provided a program for secondary school students with detailed description of the seven stages of the information search process and practical activities to guide students at each stage. *Seeking Meaning: A Process Approach to Library and Information Services* (1993) presented the theoretical framework for a process approach to library and information services that was developed in a series of studies of the information search process and offers insights into pressing problems of seeking meaning from an overabundance of information. A second edition of that book, published in 2004, incorporated recent studies and ideas including a new chapter on the implementation of a process approach to library and information services in K–12 education.

In January 2006 I officially retired to become professor emerita at the School of Communication, Information and Library Studies at Rutgers University, although I still remain active in The Rutgers Center for International Scholarship in School Libraries (CISSL). During my 20-year tenure at Rutgers my work on the information search process (ISP) was recognized as one of the most frequently cited models of information-seeking behavior in the field of library and information science. Throughout those years I continued as coordinator of the School Library Specialization in the Masters of Library and Information Science, which was ranked by *US News & World Report* in 1999 and 2006 as the number one program of its kind in the country. For a number of years I have been thinking about a culminating endeavor to bring my research on information-seeking behavior together into a publication for teachers and school librarians. I remain firmly convinced that school libraries are an essential information center in the information age school and that school librarians are primary agents for reforming schools in the 21st century.

That would have made an interesting book, but another opportunity emerged that made the book even more valuable for addressing the pressing issues facing schools in the 21st century. Two of my daughters, Leslie Maniotes and Ann Caspari, have pursued careers in areas of education, and our conversations over the years have broadened the scope of our thinking about teaching and learning.

Leslie Maniotes is a National Board Certified teacher with extensive background in curriculum development and assessment. She is a Reading Recovery certified literacy specialist with a master's degree in reading. She was trained in New Zealand and has worked as a teacher advancement trainer and university instructor. Her doctoral research, completed in 2005, on the concept of "third space" shed considerable light on ways of engaging students in learning that are central to Guided Inquiry.

Ann Caspari is a specialist in museum education with a master's degree in teaching from George Washington University. As a museum educator she does extensive training workshops with teachers and museum workers to improve learning at museums. She has an extensive background as a museum educator at the Newport Historical Society, Paul Revere House, Calvert (MD) Marine Museum, National Building Museum, and the Smithsonian Early Enrichment Center. Her expertise in the use of community resources and object-based learning expanded our understanding of the vast range of resources available for learning in 21st-century schools.

This book grew out of ongoing conversations among the three of us, usually at our beach house on the Jersey shore. When the family gathers at the beach we have time for leisurely conversations that often turn to our work, probably too often for the rest of the family. When we realized that inquiry was the dynamic at the center of each of our specializations, we began to see the tremendous potential for conceptualizing 21st-century schools. As we developed the concept of learning through Guided Inquiry, we decided to write this book together.

This book is written for the entire school community as an instructional team joining forces to provide engaging, challenging education for students in prekindergarten through secondary school. It will be of particular interest to

- educators who want to prepare students for work, citizenship, and daily living in an information-rich environment;

- educators who want to know more about inquiry as a way of learning and teaming as a way of teaching;

- teachers, school librarians, administrators, and supervisors who are initiating an inquiry approach to learning in their schools;

- teachers and school librarians who are using a project-based approach to teaching, but want to make the projects more meaningful;

- teachers and school librarians who want to implement an inquiry approach to enhance content areas of the curriculum;

- school librarians who want to involve classroom teachers and content area specialists in an inquiry approach to scaffolding information literacy throughout grade levels;

- public librarians and museum educators who want to know about an inquiry approach and their role in working with school staff and students; and

- parents who want to see their children engaged in learning and preparing for 21st-century living.

This foundational text on Guided Inquiry is organized in ten chapters. Chapter 1 introduces Guided Inquiry, considering what it is, what's new about it, and why it is pertinent for addressing the issues facing 21st-century schools. Chapter 2 presents the theory and research that is the foundation of Guided Inquiry. Chapter 3 presents new work on motivating students by connecting the curriculum to their world. Chapter 4 discusses ways for taking full advantage of varied expertise within the school and community for building instructional teams for Guided Inquiry. Chapter 5 presents a concept approach to information literacy that develops and reinforces practical information-seeking skills and strategies. Chapter 6 discusses subject area curriculum standards that are best met through Guided Inquiry. Chapter 7 provides interventions for promoting deeper learning through Guided Inquiry. Chapter 8 proposes a wide range of resources for Guided Inquiry, from the school library, to the Internet, to public libraries, museums, and the community. Chapter 9 discusses the central role of assessment in Guided Inquiry. Chapter 10 sums up important proposals presented in this book.

Many people have contributed to the ideas and content of this book, far too many to acknowledge here. We want to take this opportunity to expressly thank the research team at the Center for International Scholarship in School Libraries (CISSL) at Rutgers, particularly my wonderful colleague Ross Todd, our research associate Jannica Heinstrom, and the entire CISSL team; Randi and Peter Schmidt and the librarians and teachers at Gill St. Bernard School, who have created a systemic model of Guided Inquiry; Bridget Lydon McGrath and her students for the study of third space; Shelby Wolf for her insightful guidance; the teams of librarians and teachers in the New Jersey study of the Impact of School Libraries on Student Learning; Sue Easun and Mary Jane McNally for their insights into early drafts; and John Kuhlthau for his constant support and encouragement.

Carol C. Kuhlthau
Professor Emerita
Library and Information Science
Rutgers University

Introduction to Guided Inquiry: What Is It, What's New, Why Now?

Inquiry helps kids to think creatively. When you capture their imagination they begin to think creatively and creativity solves problems for life.
—middle school librarian

How do we educate our students to meet the demand for high levels of literacy in the technological workplace? How do we prepare our students for this global information environment? How do we enable our students to draw on the knowledge and wisdom of the past while using the technology of the present to advance new discoveries for the future? How do we prepare our students to think for themselves, make good decisions, develop expertise, and learn throughout life? These are fundamental questions for school reform in the 21st century, and they confront teachers in schools around the world. Basic to meeting these challenges is developing student competence in learning in information-laden environments and for finding meaning from a variety of sources of information. Many teachers are turning to inquiry learning in subjects across the curriculum to meet the challenge of educating their students for lifelong learning.

Guided Inquiry offers an integrated unit of inquiry, planned and guided by an instructional team of a school librarian and teachers, allowing students to gain deeper understandings of subject area curriculum content and information literacy concepts. It combines often overlooked outside resources with materials in the school library. The team guides students toward developing skills and abilities necessary for the workplace and daily living in the rapidly changing information environment of the 21st century. But how is this different from what teachers and librarians have been doing all along?

Preparing Students for a Changing World

Worldwide access to information technology has focused attention on serious questions about education in countries across the globe (Friedman, 2006). Educational leaders and policy makers are worried about the next generation of innovators and creators. Schools are faced with the overwhelming challenge of preparing students to be successful, productive citizens in

1

a changing world. Vast quantities of information fuel this global society, and the ability to locate, evaluate, and use appropriate information for creation and innovation is essential. Thoughtful educators seek ways to build student competencies for living and working with new technologies. Educators around the world are heatedly debating how to prepare students for living and working in the 21st century.

Many countries sense that they are falling behind. The United States in particular is concerned about the general level of literacy among low-achieving students and the loss of human talent through the attrition of disadvantaged students in urban schools. Kozol (2005) distressingly describes how schools for the neediest and poorest populations return again and again to an industrial age model of training students.

The challenge for the 21st-century school is to educate children for living and working in an information-rich technological environment. Three basic charges of education in a free society are to prepare students for the workplace, citizenship, and daily living. Schools need to be reconfigured for the 21st century to ensure that all children are fully prepared. To prepare students for the workplace, we must seriously consider how information technology changes the nature of work and raises new questions about how we contribute to and innovate productively in the global economy. To prepare students for citizenship, consideration must be given to the ways that information technology changes our sense of community and raises pressing questions about how we participate as an informed electorate in a democratic society. To prepare students for daily living, consideration must be given to the ways that information technology increases the complexity of everyday life and raises troubling questions about how we gain a sense of self in relation to others and experience creativity and joy in our personal lives.

Inquiry Learning

Inquiry is an approach to learning whereby students find and use a variety of sources of information and ideas to increase their understanding of a problem, topic, or issue. It requires more of them than simply answering questions or getting a right answer. It espouses investigation, exploration, search, quest, research, pursuit, and study. Inquiry does not stand alone; it engages, interests, and challenges students to connect their world with the curriculum. Although it is often thought of as an individual pursuit, it is enhanced by involvement with a community of learners, each learning from the other in social interaction. However, without some guidance it can be daunting.

Guiding Students' Inquiry

Students gain competence by being guided through an inquiry process by teachers and librarians at each grade level. Guided Inquiry, as we shall see, is grounded in sound research findings and built on solid professional practice. Through Guided Inquiry students gain the ability to use tools and resources for learning in and beyond the information age while they are learning the content of the curriculum and meeting subject area curriculum standards. Guided Inquiry instructional teams help students develop research competency and subject knowledge as well as foster motivation, reading comprehension, language development, writing ability, cooperative learning, and social skills. All of these have been identified as essential for successful lifelong learning.

Guided Inquiry requires careful planning, close supervision, ongoing assessment, and targeted intervention by an instructional team of school librarians and teachers through the inquiry process that gradually leads students toward independent learning. An integrated unit of inquiry is planned and guided by such an instructional team. Its ultimate goal is to develop independent learners who know how to expand their knowledge and expertise through skilled use of a variety of information sources employed both inside and outside the school. Resources inside the school, such as library materials, databases, and other selected sources, are supplemented and expanded by public libraries, local community resources, museums, and the Internet.

What's New About Guided Inquiry?

Term papers and research reports have been standard school assignments seemingly forever. In some cases they are important culminating activities for a course of study. But far too often they are merely extraneous assignments added on after the "real" teaching of the curriculum has been accomplished. If they somehow improved students' ability and skills in academic work, particularly for success in college, that has been sufficient.

Alas, many students suspected as much, viewing these assignments as academic exercises without much internal value or real-life application. This attitude became abundantly clear in the course of the lead author's information- seeking studies: Students regularly informed her that the purpose of a research assignment was to learn how to do a bibliography or the format of a paper for college (Kuhlthau, 1988b). Still, as one student reflected, "Now that I think about it, I guess it was a missed opportunity. I thought it was just one more needless school exercise. If I knew I'd find out something of my own that was interesting I could have given more time. I did it all the last night." In the past decade, we have seen research transformed from a traditional academic exercise into an important part of everyday living. In a different series of studies, a securities analyst attributed his success to viewing his work as "writing research papers for a living." His work involves investigating background information on an industry and a particular company within that industry, tracking current information and reporting with what he calls "an angle that provides value for his clients." The lawyers in that study saw extensive research seeking as essential for constructing a strategy in a particularly complex trial.

Yet for many students, school seems disconnected from their lives. Project-based learning has been employed in some schools to motivate students. This approach seeks to get students involved in an extended project that requires gathering information to build something. Project-based learning is a good step in the right direction, at times successful in engaging students in deeper learning. However, it falls short in two respects. First, it overemphasizes product and underemphasizes the learning process. Second, students are frequently left to their own devices, and when parents step in, many end up doing the actual research.

Educators who use the KWL framework (Ogle, 1986), like those using project-based learning, are well on their way to teaching through Guided Inquiry. They have their students ask, "What do I know?" (K); "What do I want to learn?" (W); and "What did I learn?" (L). These questions are the seeds of a constructivist approach. Guided Inquiry simply extends this model by insisting that students think about the facts and ideas they are encountering. The instructional team pushes the KWL framework further, to incorporate, "How do I find out?"; "How do I share what I learned?"; and "What will I do next time?" Through focusing on finding new information, learning it, and connecting it to what students already know, the team leads each student through the joint processes of constructing new knowledge and sharing it with others. Asking, "What will I do next time?" fosters reflection that enables transference to other situations and promotes the metacognition of higher order thinking. This reflection incorporates thinking about both *content* (What did I learn?), and *process* (How did I learn?), so that students gain a deeper appreciation of information seeking and use. (See Figure 1.1.)

Extending KWL Questions for Guided Inquiry

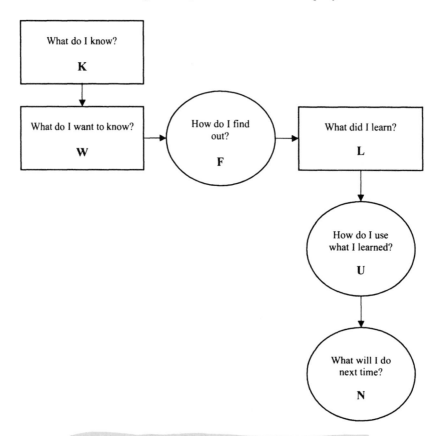

Figure 1.1. Extending KWL Questions for Guided Inquiry.

Inquiry learning in general emphasizes those questions and ideas that motivate students to want to learn more and create ways to share what they have learned. Guided Inquiry raises the bar even further to move students to a higher level of thinking and learning by focusing instructive interventions at each stage of the inquiry process. The instructional team concentrates on what students are thinking, feeling, and doing as they are learning. The end product becomes a natural way of sharing their learning with the rest of the students in their learning community.

What's the Difference Between Guided Inquiry and Other Types of Instruction?

Guided Inquiry is a preparation for lifelong learning, not just preparation for a test. While it is important that students be able to show what they know, many test-oriented approaches are counterproductive in that they do not foster the lasting connections essential for a person educated in a rapidly changing information environment. Inquiry learning is effective for preparing students to think deeply about a subject so that they are able to succeed in tests authentic to the learning situation. Guided Inquiry targets assessments to the learner and the situation as it is integrated into the process. The result is lasting learning that has meaning and application in students' lives.

Inquiry is a way of learning the content of the curriculum. Guided Inquiry is integrated into the content of the curriculum; it is not a subject in and of itself. It has the instructional team of teachers, librarians, and other specialists to enhance subject content through their respective expertise, making it more interesting, relevant, and thought provoking. Students are actively engaged in the subject content, motivating them to pursue important questions and attain a deeper understanding of that content.

In Guided Inquiry, the content of the curriculum is connected to the student's world through thoughtful planning and adaptability. The instructional team plans and implements guidance for students, with each member contributing his or her special expertise. The team works in concert to provide the full range of learning for students rather than each member tackling a particular piece in isolation from the others. Each team member collaborates on all aspects of learning, from the initial planning of the unit through all stages of implementation, adapting as students progress.

Guided Inquiry incorporates transferable information literacy concepts into the inquiry process. It does not teach isolated information skills that are difficult for students to recall and apply. Too much of the mechanics of searching and resources at the beginning of research discourages students and distracts them from the interesting ideas and questions that motivate them to learn (Kuhlthau, 1985b). Rather than attempting to teach all there is to know about information seeking prior to the assignment, Guided Inquiry incorporates information location, evaluation, and use concepts throughout the research process. Lasting information literacy is developed in practice when both information concepts and search skills in the inquiry process can be recalled and applied as needed.

Students are involved in every stage of the learning process, from selecting what to investigate, to formulating a focused perspective, to presenting their learning in the final product. There is rarely a correct answer to a prescribed question imposed by the teacher or text. Instead, Guided Inquiry incorporates reflection throughout the process, with the end product as evidence of knowledge construction and deeper understanding. (See Figure 1.2, p. 6)

In Guided Inquiry students, teachers, and librarians collaborate and work together on ideas. Students work as a community of learners, helping and learning from each other rather than as individuals working exclusively on private tasks. The teachers and librarians do the same. It can be difficult to script how the inquiry process will progress, but we will help.

What Guided Inquiry Is Not and Is	
Guided Inquiry Is Not . . .	**Guided Inquiry Is . . .**
Preparation solely for the test	Preparation for lifelong learning
An add-on subject	Integrated into content areas
Isolated information skills	Transferable information concepts
Relying on one textbook	Using a variety of sources
Finding answers to a prescribed question	Involving students in every stage of the learning, from planning to the final product
Curriculum without meaning to students	Curriculum connected to the students' world
Individual students working exclusively on solitary tasks	A community of learners working together
Solely teacher directed	Students and teachers collaborating
Overemphasis on the end product	Emphasis on the process and product

Figure 1.2. What Guided Inquiry Is Not and Is.

What Are the Benefits for Students, Teachers, and Librarians?

There can be no question that Guided Inquiry requires much time, attention, and commitment. Why make the investment?

Guided Inquiry creates an environment that motivates students to learn by providing opportunities for them to construct their own meaning and develop deep understanding. This approach engages all students, not just those who have already shown that they are academically inclined. In the Center for International Scholarship in School Libraries (CISSL) study of student learning through inquiry projects conducted by Todd, Kuhlthau, and Heinstrom (2005), a wide range of students participated, including those classified with learning disabilities, students at risk for dropping out of school, and ESL (English as a Second Language) students. Every one of these students was shown to benefit from learning through inquiry. They all gained a sense of their own learning process by successfully pursuing a project from start to finish. But more important, they learned strategies and skills transferable to other inquiry projects and other situations in which information would be needed. Independence in research and learning, development of a variety of skills, and social as well as language and reading skills are embedded in the Guided Inquiry approach. (See Figure 1.3.)

Benefits for Students
• Develop social, language, and reading skills
• Construct their own meaning
• Gain independence in research and learning
• Experience a high level of motivation and engagement
• Learn strategies and skills transferable to other inquiry projects

Figure 1.3. Benefits for Students.

Teachers and librarians can also benefit from Guided Inquiry in a number of important ways. As they share responsibility in an instructional team, they also share in the expertise of their team members, as well as in the satisfaction of accomplishment and the success of even their most difficult students. There is no limit to the size of the team. Basic pairing of school librarian and subject area teachers can be expanded to include other staff members such as the technology teacher, literacy and reading specialist, study skills teacher, and special subject specialist. Outside experts can also be called upon, such as public librarians, children's and young adult librarians, museum educators, and community experts. Teachers benefit by the enhancement of content areas of the curriculum. Librarians increase their professional contribution to the school by being involved in meaningful learning with students. The library is an active learning environment in which information literacy and curriculum standards are met simultaneously. Guided Inquiry allows for brainstorming and planning with more creativity and hence more satisfaction for the expert as well as the students. (See Figures 1.4 and 1.5.)

Benefits for Teachers

- Share responsibility in the instructional team
- Share expertise of the team members
- Teach content and information skills simultaneously
- Brainstorm and plan with more creativity
- Experience enhancement of content areas of the curriculum

Figure 1.4. Benefits for Teachers.

Benefits for Librarians

- Involvement in meaningful learning with students
- Shared responsibility with instructional team
- Library becoming an active learning environment
- Information literacy being taught in context
- Increased level of professional contribution

Figure 1.5. Benefits for Librarians.

What Are the Benefits for Administrators and Parents?

Administrators, including superintendents, principals, supervisors, and curriculum coordinators, set the tone of the learning environment and provide the climate for the education of students. They provide the funding and support for promoting educational programs and encouraging methods of teaching and ways of learning that match their outlook and meet their goals. Guided Inquiry provides opportunities for administrators who are seeking ways to make a school more in touch with the needs of 21st-century living and working. (See Figure 1.6.)

Benefits for Administrators

- Fosters systemic change to improve learning
- Promotes constructivist approach to learning
- Achieves multiple curricular goals
- Fosters collaborative climate for team instruction
- Changes school to meet needs of 21st-century workplace

Figure 1.6. Benefits for Administrators.

Parents often feel overwhelmed by the responsibility of assisting their children and teenagers with research assignments. In many traditional research assignments students are left on their own through much of the process. Concerned parents fill in as best they can. Guided Inquiry puts the responsibility back with the educators, where it belongs. Parents are aware that this is fairer to all students. It takes the burden of teaching from parents and places it squarely in the hands of the instructional team and the student. Guided Inquiry makes students more interested in school and learning, and parents are well rewarded when they see their children becoming responsible learners. (See Figure 1.7.)

Benefits for Parents

- Places responsibility with educators
- Is fairer for all students
- Takes away burden of teaching research
- Enables observation of children becoming independent learners
- Makes school more interesting and relevant

Figure 1.7. Benefits for Parents.

What Are the Benefits for Me?

Raising the Standard of My Research Assignments

Motivation and interest are key elements in inquiry learning. Students use a wide range of sources of information to explore ideas rather than being confined to one textbook of predigested facts. They form their own understandings through conversation and writing. They work with other students to formulate their ideas but are encouraged to create deep understanding for themselves. They gain a sense of ownership and accomplishment in the work they are producing that gradually leads to competence and expertise.

Increasing the Depth and Breadth of What I Can Offer

Guided Inquiry allows students to gain a greater understanding of subject area content and information literacy concepts. At the same time students are developing competency in reading, writing, and speaking, and in turn gaining social skills through interacting, cooperating, and collaborating with other students. In addition, they are learning *how* to learn in an information rich environment. Students are engaged in five kinds of learning: curriculum content, information literacy, learning processes, literacy competencies, and social abilities. Any subject area content can be applied to Guided Inquiry as long as the subject involves an inquiry that is deeper than mere fact finding. (See Figure 1.8.)

Five Kinds of Learning in the Inquiry Process	
1. Curriculum content	fact finding, interpreting, and synthesizing
2. Information literacy	concepts for locating, evaluating, and using
3. Learning how to learn	initiating, selecting, exploring, focusing, collecting, and presenting
4. Literacy competence	reading, writing, speaking, and listening
5. Social skills	interacting, cooperating, and collaborating

Figure 1.8. Five Kinds of Learning in the Inquiry Process.

Role of Assessment in Guided Inquiry

Assessment is the means by which the instructional team knows how to guide students through the inquiry process. It is folded into the learning process, providing evidence of problems and indications of when intervention is needed. In particular, longitudinal assessment, determining what students know and can do over an extended period of time, offers extensive information about students' progress, incorporating content area learning, information literacy, learning approaches, literacy skills, and social abilities. Assessment also supports the continuity of Guided Inquiry from primary grades through secondary school.

Research on the Impact of School Libraries on Student Learning

There is substantial evidence that students benefit from learning through school libraries. A review of some of the major research on the impact of school libraries on student learning indicates the value of engaging students in Guided Inquiry.

During the last half of the 20th century a growing body of research demonstrated the impact of school libraries on academic achievement. In the 1960s Mary Gaver (1963) of Rutgers University compared the test scores of students in schools with centralized school libraries with the scores of students in schools without libraries. The study, conducted in 271 schools in 13 states, found that the test scores of students in schools with centralized libraries managed by qualified librarians were higher than those of students in schools without libraries or qualified librarians. However, the volume of data generated by this study was difficult to calculate with the technology of the day. By the 1980s computers had made massive calculation possible, as demonstrated by SchoolMatch, a national commercial database of school statistics. In a National Public Radio interview, SchoolMatch executive William Bainbridge reported that spending on school libraries was the single factor with the greatest influence on students' school performance.

Inspired by the SchoolMatch results, Keith Curry Lance and his colleagues (2001) at the Colorado State Library conducted extensive, large-scale, statewide studies throughout the 1990s based on the study design developed by Gaver, using schools rather than students as the unit of analysis. By 2005 the Colorado study model had been replicated and elaborated upon in more than a dozen states. Collectively these studies have examined the impact of libraries in approximately 8,700 schools with enrollments totaling more than 2.6 million students. The studies elaborated upon the original Colorado study model by identifying specific activities of school staff that constituted playing an instructional role.

The Lance teams found that "across states and grade levels, test scores correlated positively and statistically significantly with library staff and collection size; library staff activities related to learning and teaching, information access and delivery, and program administration; and the availability of networked computers, both in the library and elsewhere in the school, that provide access to library catalogs, databases, and the World Wide Web." The cause-and-effect claim associated with these correlations was strengthened by the reliability of the relationships between key library variables (i.e., staffing, collection size, spending) and test scores when other school and community conditions were taken into account. These studies revealed that the "two most consistent predictors of test scores, when all potential predictors were considered, were the prevalence of students from poor households and the level of development of the school library" (Callison, 2005). It is clear from these studies that learning in high-quality school libraries is of considerable benefit to students.

At the First International Research Symposium sponsored by The Center for International Scholarship in School Libraries at Rutgers University (CISSL) in April 2005, Lance gave a keynote address entitled, "Enough Already." He stressed the need to move beyond studies of correlation with standardized test scores to research that reveals ways to assess, intervene in, and improve student learning in school libraries. CISSL has taken up just such research on the impact of school libraries on student learning and the development programs of Guided Inquiry (Todd, Kuhlthau, and Heinstrom, 2005). In a series of studies, the CISSL team has developed an assessment tool called "Student Learning through Inquiry Measure" (SLIM), which assesses the progress of students' learning and indicates when and what intervention is needed. Chapter 8 presents a full discussion of SLIM as an important assessment tool for Guided Inquiry.

Leaving the 20th Century Behind

Much has been written about rethinking and redefining schools to accomplish the mission of educating the next generation for living and working in an information-laden society. To address this critical need, a number of school reform advocates have called for organizing around an inquiry approach to learning. However, few educators have recognized the power of the school library as an integral element in designing the information age school. Recent studies have shown a significant impact of school libraries on student learning (Lance et al., 2001; Todd and Kuhlthau, 2005a, 2005b). Guided Inquiry describes how the school library and the school librarian are employed to implement an instructional team approach for meeting curriculum objectives in a variety of subject areas while developing the necessary research competence. The school librarian brings resource and research expertise to the instructional team. Other members of the instructional team bring specializations; all combine to provide a powerful learning environment for students. An instructional team approach to Guided Inquiry incorporates multiple ways of knowing and provides students with essential competencies for a changing information society. The school librarian has the expertise to provide a wide range of high-quality resources and the knowledge to guide students in locating, evaluating, and using resources for constructing deep learning.

The configuration of the 21st-century school is quite different from its 20th-century industrial age counterpart. The old model, in which one teacher and one class of students was the norm, is surely past its prime. The information age and the future call for a team approach, each member bringing his or her expertise to a collaborative learning environment. Research competency and subject knowledge in the context of fostering cooperative learning, reading comprehension, language development, and social skills are needed.

Through Guided Inquiry students see school learning and real life meshed in integral ways. They develop higher order thinking and strategies for seeking meaning and competencies for creating and innovating. Twenty-first-century schools are challenged to develop that human talent by coupling the rich resources of the school library with those of the surrounding community and the wider world.

The Theory and Research Basis
for Guided Inquiry

2

After several years teachers saw that it [Guided Inquiry] was transforming their teaching.
Teachers see that the program is important enough to make it systemic, to take it to the
next step. Wow! This has changed the course of our school instructional program.
— principal

Every educator has a theory of learning that forms the basis of the instruction and the learning environment he or she provides for students. While you read this chapter, reflect on your own theory of learning. Although your theory of learning may not be overtly articulated, nevertheless it underlies all you do with your students. It is important to examine your own theory of learning and determine what principles underlie your teaching. How do you view learning taking place? What are your teaching methods based on? What kind of learning environment do you strive to provide for your students?

This chapter presents the underlying theory and research base for Guided Inquiry. First we discuss the constructivist theory of learning, which is drawn from a long tradition of educational theory, research, and practice. Then we present studies of students' experiences in the process of research assignments that are specifically related to the inquiry process. Finally, we summarize the six fundamental principles of Guided Inquiry.

Constructivist Approach to Learning

Guided Inquiry has a solid theoretical foundation grounded in the constructivist approach to learning. It is based on the work of major educational theorists and researchers, including Dewey, Bruner, Kelly, Vygotsky, and Piaget. Taken together these theorists have provided fundamental principles for educating students that have lasting and sustaining value for designing instruction. Too often teachers are caught in the pendulum of trends that discard the wisdom of the past for the flash of the new. Although we need to be open to innovation and new ideas, we must recognize the substantial body of accumulated knowledge that sustains the education profession. The constructivist approach described in this chapter is based on established principles drawn from these theorists that have important implications for designing learning environments for 21st-century schools.

We may think of two general approaches to learning: a transmission approach, in which learning is viewed as something the teacher or text does to the student, and a constructivist approach, in which the student is involved in an active process of constructing deep understanding. A transmission approach to teaching emphasizes finding the right answer, memorizing specific facts, and repackaging information. Instruction is structured to transmit specific facts and train in precise skills. A constructivist approach builds knowledge by engaging students in stimulating encounters with information and ideas. Students learn by constructing their own understanding of these encounters and by building on what they already know to form a personal perspective of the world. Construction is an active, ongoing process of learning that continues throughout life.

Constructivist Theory of John Dewey

The underlying assumption of this book is that learning is a process of construction based on the educational theory of John Dewey. Dewey, an early constructivist, articulated a philosophy of education that would prepare students for work, citizenship, and life in a free society. Dewey's philosophy of education for a democratic society is surprisingly fresh and relevant today as we strive to design schools for the 21st century. His most comprehensive work, *Democracy and Education*, first published in 1915, provides the foundation for inquiry learning. It incorporates the experience, action, and thinking of the whole child. Dewey explained that, "education is not an affair of telling and being told but an active and constructive process." He cautioned that, "The accumulation and acquisition of information for purposes of reproduction in recitation and examination is made too much of. Knowledge in the sense of information means working capital, the indispensable resources of further inquiry of finding out or learning more things" (Dewey, 1915, p. 158). Guided Inquiry is based on this concept of information as "working capital" for constructing understanding and knowledge for each learner.

Dewey's familiar motto, "learning by doing," is only part of the picture. Reflection on the activity is the other essential component. Dewey described learning as a creative process of inquiry, beginning with a suggestion caused by new information that raises a question or problem. Through reflection, a guiding idea is formed that leads to the quest for understanding. There is reflection in every stage or phase of the learning process.

In *How We Think* (1933), Dewey elaborated on the concept of inquiry in his description of the phases of reflective thinking (see Figure 2.1). The first phase, *suggestion*, is a state of doubt due to an incomplete situation and is characterized by perplexity and confusion. The second phase, called *intellectualization*, involves conceptualizing the problem or question and anticipating possible solutions. In the third phase, a *guiding idea* is formed to direct the collection of factual material to define and clarify the problem. In the fourth phase, called *reasoning*, the guiding idea is made more precise and consistent by familiarity with a wider range of information. The fifth phase, called *action*, involves taking a stand on the elaborated idea to bring about results that resolve the initial state of doubt through understanding (Kuhlthau, 2004, p. 16).

Dewey's Phases of Reflective Thinking	
Phase	**Definition**
Suggestion	Doubt due to incomplete situation
Intellectualization	Conceptualizing the problem
Guiding idea (hypothesis)	Tentative interpretation
Reasoning	Interpretation with more precise facts
Action	Idea tested by overt or imaginative action

Source: Kuhlthau (2001, p. 16)

Figure 2.1. Dewey's Phases of Reflective Thinking.

Dewey explains that facts, data, and information arouse ideas that enable the learner to make inferences from what he or she already knows that lead to deeper understanding. The process of creating understanding for oneself evokes feelings of doubt and uncertainty on one side, joy and confidence on the other, and a whole range of emotions in between.

The Interplay of Thinking, Feeling, and Acting

Notice that the thread woven through these theories beginning with Dewey's reflective thinking is that learning begins with confusion and uncertainty. Learners actively reflect on the new information to form their own ideas throughout the learning process, which gradually leads to deep understanding. Learning is an emotional as well as a thinking and acting process. These theorists clearly acknowledge the complexity of the holistic experience of the learning process that is often overlooked in our schools.

George Kelly's Personal Construct Theory (1963) describes the emotional experience of constructing meaning from new information. The information is assimilated in a series of phases, beginning with confusion. Confusion increases as inconsistencies and incompatibilities between the information and the constructs the person already holds are confronted. As confusion mounts, it frequently causes doubt about one's ability to assimilate the new information. The disruption caused by the new ideas may become so threatening that the new information is discarded and construction abandoned. At this point, Kelly proposes another alternative to move the process of construction along. As in Dewey's guiding idea, the person may form a tentative hypothesis to move toward incorporating the new construct into the existing system of personally held constructs.

Jerome Bruner's studies of perception further verify and refine the constructive view of the nature of human thinking and learning. Bruner was influenced by Piaget's research on the concept of schema, which is akin to Kelly's notion of construct. *Schema* is an integrated, organized representation of past behavior and experience that guides individuals in reconstructing new information. Bruner's (1977) research confirms that we are actively involved in making sense of the world around us rather than being passive receivers of information. Bruner elaborates on the basic concepts in the constructive sequences of both Dewey and Kelly. Taken together, the theories of Dewey, Kelly, and Bruner provide a vivid explanation of construction and learning. These theorists agree that emotions play a significant role in directing thinking and action throughout the constructive process of learning.

Recent brain research in neuroscience further supports this holistic view of learning that the brain runs on emotions that drive thoughts and actions to seek meaning through patterns and connections. An enriched learning environment that is challenging, social, and fun increases brain waves. Guided Inquiry addresses students' emotions as well as the thoughts and actions that lead to deep learning. Students are challenged and engaged in their own quest for understanding and knowledge, which prepares them for learning throughout their lives. Guided Inquiry strives to provide that challenging, social, and fun enriched learning environment.

Research Base for Guided Inquiry

Now that we've considered general learning theories that support Guided Inquiry, let's turn to the research that specifically explains the approach. Guided Inquiry is grounded in the constructivist principles of major educational theorists and in the research on the information search process of students. The Kuhlthau research on the process of learning from a variety of sources also forms the basis for Guided Inquiry.

Too often schools plunge into the "latest program," designed on someone's "good idea" with little or no research base. It may sound impressive but is often superficial, overlooking the important findings on how students learn. Guided Inquiry is based on extensive studies of students learning through research assignments in school libraries. This research over the past 20 years has enabled us to understand a great deal about students' experiences in the inquiry process. It grew out of a practical problem that Kuhlthau confronted as a school librarian. Her research is explained in the next section of this chapter. Was the library providing an environment for constructing new knowledge? Or was it merely providing materials and resources?

Kuhlthau's studies answered some of these questions. They revealed different thoughts, feelings, and actions at each stage in the inquiry process. The stages are described in the model of the information search process (ISP). The ISP model was originally developed in a study of secondary students in the early 1980s and was confirmed and expanded in successive studies, which revealed this to be a common experience of not only students but people in the workplace and other areas of life in which extensive information seeking and learning was involved.

A comprehensive summary of this research is provided in *Seeking Meaning: A Process Approach to Library and Information Services* (1993; 2nd ed. 2004). The second edition incorporates the implementation studies in K–12 schools that formed the basis for the Guided Inquiry approach. Recent studies of inquiry learning conducted by the Center for International Scholarship in School Libraries (CISSL) at Rutgers University (Todd, Kuhlthau, and Heinstrom, 2005) found the ISP model applied in technological information environments as well. The ISP model incorporates reflection and thinking that is easily overlooked when using electronic information. We now have insight into the inquiry process based on solid research, which enables us to design instruction for guiding students in their learning.

An Important Discovery

An important discovery in this research is that there are distinct stages in the inquiry process, and some stages are more difficult for students than others. Inquiry is initiated by someone who has something that needs investigation, a fundamental question, pressing issue, or troubling problem that requires further information. This is followed by selection of a general area or topic to address the investigation. Two stages—exploration and formulation—follow, during which important learning from information occurs. This is followed by the collection of specific information and facts, which leads to completing the task and preparing to share with others in the presentation stage.

The stages of exploration and formulation are usually an unpleasant surprise for students, and sometimes for teachers and librarians as well. Too often they expect to move directly from selecting the general topic for investigation to gathering and collecting information for completing the assignment. These studies show that the exploration and formulation stages are difficult and confusing for many students. They are encountering lots of new ideas that often conflict with what they already know and seem incompatible with each other, as Kelly described in his Personal Construct Theory. However, it is during exploration that the most significant learning takes place in the inquiry process. This is a crucial time in Guided Inquiry for teachers and librarians to intervene to guide their students through reflection and thinking. Throughout the inquiry process information and facts are reflected upon and synthesized to promote deep understanding and extensive learning.

Uncertainty is the beginning of learning. It is an important concept that underlies the inquiry process. Information often initially increases the sense of uncertainty rather than reducing it. Students need to become aware of their own uncertainty and learn to work through ideas that lead to understanding and decrease uncertainty. Learning begins with uncertainty and is driven by the desire to seek meaning (Kuhlthau, 2004, pp. 89–105). Once students learn this process they can adapt to a wide range of information-laden tasks in life. As one of my case study subjects explained, "I'll worry about a paper because things don't fall into place but it is not the kind of thing I'll lose sleep over. I've learned to accept that this is the way it works. Tomorrow I'll read this over and some parts will fall into place and some still won't . . . . The mind doesn't take everything and put it into order automatically and that's it. Understanding that is the biggest help" (2004, p. 77).

Kuhlthau's Model of the Information Search Process

In training institutes and workshops on the ISP in inquiry projects, school librarians and teachers conduct their own research and reflect on the stages they are going through. They become aware of how they feel during these stages, how they work through these stages, and what strategies they use to help them complete their tasks. This prepares them for designing interventions for guiding their students' inquiry. It is important to recognize that there is a vast difference between a simple question that may be addressed in a routine search and a complex issue that requires more extensive research. A complex issue is one that the searcher doesn't know much about and that requires significant learning. It is during these complex tasks that require extensive searching and learning that the stages of the ISP are commonly experienced.

While you read this section, think about how you do research and your own experience researching a topic or problem that is important to you. How do you work through a complex issue? Have you experienced these stages in your research? Perhaps you have recently taken a course that required a written paper or oral presentation. Do you recognize the stages described in the model of the ISP as similar to your own experience? Reflect on your own experience in research and consider how your experience might help you guide your students in a similar learning process.

Students' experiences in the process of inquiry have been carefully documented in a series of empirical studies (Kuhlthau, 2004). In a recent study of inquiry learning in ten schools in New Jersey, we found the same pattern of students' feelings, with confusion and uncertainty increasing during the exploration stage in the technological information environment of today's schools (Todd, Kuhlthau, and Heinstrom, 2005). In fact, advances in information technology have made the exploration and formulation stages more difficult for students to work through on their own and more critical for them to learn to manage. These studies also show that as students move beyond the formulation stage of the inquiry process, their interest increases along with their confidence. They become more engaged and interested as they construct their own understanding.

The model of the ISP describes feelings, thoughts, and actions of students involved in complex inquiry tasks in which they are required to construct their own understandings. The seven process stages are initiation, selection, exploration, formulation, collection, presentation, and assessment (see Figure 2.2).

In the first stage, it is usually the teacher who *initiates* the inquiry process by announcing a unit of study that will require extensive research from multiple sources, to be accomplished over a number of weeks. The task of the first stage is to prepare for the decision of selecting a topic. Students often feel apprehensive and uncertain about what is expected of them. Some students in the studies described feeling depressed and bogged down and overwhelmed at the amount of work ahead.

In the second stage, *selection,* students choose their general topic, aspect of, or question about the class project that they will be working on. The possible topics may be weighed against the criteria of personal interest, assignment requirements, information available, and time allotted. During the period when students are uncertain about what topic to choose, they may become somewhat anxious. After they decide on a research topic, they often experience a brief sense of elation, followed by apprehension at the extent of the task ahead.

During the third stage, *exploration,* the students' task is to explore information with the intent of finding a focus. Students need to become informed about the general topic and to identify possible ways to focus it. As they find information about their topic, they frequently become confused by the inconsistencies and incompatibilities they encounter. Sources are often inconsistent and are incompatible with a student's preconceived notions about the topic. The feeling of confusion can become quite threatening, and some students want to drop their topics at this point. For most students, this is the most difficult stage of the research process. They are confronted with the complicated task of working through their own ideas and constructing new knowledge to prepare to form a focused perspective to pursue. In this confusing time of exploring for ideas, students can easily become frustrated and discouraged.

The *formulation* stage is a time to form a focus for the research from the information on the general topic found in the variety of sources students are consulting. Students need to identify possible ways to focus their topic to center their information gathering. The four criteria used to select a topic may again be employed to choose a focus. The focus may be of personal interest, meet the requirements of the assignment, be able to be researched in available materials, and be able to be accomplished within the time allotted. However, it is likely that one of these will take precedence over the others as a criterion for formulating a focused perspective.

Model of the Information Search Process

	Initiation	Selection	Exploration	Formulation	Collection	Presentation	Assessment
Feelings (Affective)	Uncertainty	Optimism	Confusion Frustration Doubt	Clarity	Sense of direction/ confidence	Satisfaction or disappointment	Sense of accomplishment
Thoughts (Cognitive)	Vague ————————————→ Focused				Increased interest		Increased self-awareness
Actions (Physical)	Seeking relevant information ————————————→ Seeking pertinent information						
	Exploring				Documenting		

Source: Kuhlthau (2004, p. 82)

Figure 2.2. Model of the Information Search Process.

The *collection* stage follows naturally after formulation as a time for supporting and extending the focus to prepare to present new understandings. The task in this stage is to gather information that defines, extends, and supports the focus. Students' confidence and interest increase along with their sense of ownership and developing expertise.

The *presentation* stage is the culmination of the inquiry process, when the learning is prepared to share with others. During presentation students are usually satisfied with the way they have progressed. They may, however, feel disappointed that their work has not met their expectations. These feelings form the basis for assessing what went well and what went wrong and how to approach inquiry in the future. Reflection and self-assessment is an important component of the inquiry process.

In the *assessment* stage both students and teachers judge what was learned about content and process and what further learning is needed. Assessment is an important part of inquiry learning. The task of this stage is to reflect on the inquiry process and to think about what worked and what problems were encountered and what students will do in the future. This assessment stage should not be confused with routine assessments performed by the Guided Inquiry team and student at each stage of the process. This stage is an opportunity to reflect on the process as a whole. More information about the important role assessment plays throughout the process can be found in chapter 8.

Recent studies of the ISP in work tasks reveal that even expert workers experience the stages of the ISP when they are confronted with complex tasks or projects that require new information and considerable learning and construction (Kuhlthau, 2004). (See Figure 2.3.) The findings of these studies provide insight into what is important for planning Guided Inquiry to prepare students for the information intensive workplace as well as learning in school.

Fact Finding or Deep Understanding

In Louise Limberg's (1997) studies of Swedish high school students, she found that the students she studied took three different approaches to the same research assignment, with three very different outcomes. The first approach was fact finding. Students using this approach accumulated numerous unconnected facts. The second approach was looking for the right or wrong answer. Students using this approach sought a definite answer to a specific question. The third approach was synthesizing the facts to gain a deeper understanding of the topic or question. Students using this approach delved into the factual material to form their own view of the topic (Limberg and Alexandersson, 2003).

In a study of students doing inquiry projects in ten schools in New Jersey by the Center for International Scholarship in School Libraries (CISSL) at Rutgers University (Todd, Kuhlthau, and Heinstrom, 2005), students took similar approaches to an inquiry assignment: fact finding or deep understanding. Students using a fact finding approach produced projects that merely restated facts from the information they had gathered. Students assuming a deep understanding approach produced projects that reflected learning from the facts they had gathered. This study found that the approach students assumed did not relate to their grade level, academic ability, or subject area. Yet there was a clear difference in outcome, with some students only listing facts and some showing deep thinking and learning from the facts they had collected. There are clear implications that the expectations and instructions of teachers and librarians are an important element in fostering deep understanding in inquiry learning.

Todd's (1995) study of the information seeking of adolescent girls found that the girls' objective for seeking information affected the outcome of their information-seeking task. He

Progression and Development of Kuhlthau's Information Search Process		
Date	Title of Research Report*	Significance
1985	A Process Approach to Library Skills Instruction	First study of the ISP with 25 HS students
1985	An Emerging Theory of Library Instruction	Process is important in teaching research
1988	Perceptions of the Information Search Process in Libraries: A Study of Changes from High School Through College	Transference of skills from high school to college: a survey study
1988	Longitudinal Case Studies of the Information Search Process of Users in Libraries	In depth case study of six students from high school through college
1988	Meeting the Information Needs of Children and Young Adults: Basing Library Media Programs on Developmental States	Connecting cognitive-developmental stages to learning in libraries
1989	The Information Search Process of High-, Middle-, and Low-Achieving High School Seniors	Large scale examination of the ISP high school seniors
1989	Information Search Process: A Summary of Research and Implications for School Library Media Programs	Practical application using the model of the ISP in schools
1990	Validating A Model of the Search Process: A Comparison of Academic, Public, and School Library Users	Confirmation of the ISP in various types of libraries
1991	Inside the Search Process: Information Seeking from the User's Perspective	Highly cited article on cognitive and affective aspect of information seeking
1993	Implementing a Process Approach to Information Skills: A Study Identifying Indicators of Success in Library Media Programs	Identifies inhibitors and enablers of implementing the ISP in K–12 contexts
1993	A Principle of Uncertainty for Information Seeking	Explanation of the impact of emotion on the ISP
1994	Students and the Information Search Process: Zones of Intervention for Librarians	Introduction of critical moments where students need assistance and guidance
1996	The Concept of a Zone of Intervention for Identifying the Role of Intermediaries in the Information Search Process	Develops a "Zone of Intervention"
1997	Learning in Digital Libraries: An Information Search Process Approach	Information technology and the ISP, the problem of seeking meaning from abundance of information
1999	Opportunities for Student Learning in Library Power Schools	Using library for inquiry learning
1999	Accommodating the User's Information Search Process: Challenges for Information Retrieval System Designers	Implication of ISP for information system design
1999	The Role of Experience in the Information Search Process of an Early Career Information Worker: Perceptions of Uncertainty, Complexity, Construction and Sources	Comparison of novice/expert use of ISP in the workplace
1999	Information Seeking for Learning: A Study of Librarians Perceptions of Learning in School Libraries	ISP of students in science projects
2001	Information Search Process of Lawyers: A Call for "Just for Me" Information Services	Evidence of ISP in the workplace and need for creating meaning
2001	The Information Search Process (ISP) A Search for Meaning Rather Than Answers	Uncovers problem of seeking meaning from information
2001	Rethinking Libraries for the Information Age School: Vital Roles in Inquiry Learning	Consideration of changes in schools to prepare students for ISP in workplace
2004	Zones of intervention in the Information Search Process: Vital Roles for Librarians	ISP in the context of education and the workplace that indicate new roles for librarians
2006	Information Literacy through Guided Inquiry: Preparing Students for the 21st Century	Guided Inquiry for preparing students for information environment

*See references for the full citation.

Figure 2.3. Progression of Kuhlthau's Information Search Process.

identified five objectives for seeking information, each resulting in a different outcome: to get a complete picture, to get a changed picture, to get a clearer picture, to get a verified picture, or to get a position in a picture. This study revealed that what students expect to accomplish in their information seeking has an impact on the outcome. Different expectations result in different outcomes.

In Guided Inquiry the main objective is to go beyond fact finding to synthesize and assimilate facts to construct new ideas and deep understanding. It's not just fact finding, but rather active interpretation and learning. The instructional team helps students to gain a clear objective beyond fact finding. Students are led to interpret facts and in some way share their learning and new understandings. We have seen that the ISP model describes more complex information-seeking situations in which a simple answer or a list of facts does not resolve the issue. Complex information seeking requires considerable construction to assimilate new information into prior knowledge. The inquiry process may begin with fact finding, but the student is required to interpret the facts for deep learning to take place. In Guided Inquiry students are led to consider how facts fit together, what story they tell, and what questions they raise.

Students' Perspectives on the Inquiry Process

The stages of the information search process provide insight into what students experience in the inquiry process. The inquiry process described in this book is Kuhlthau's ISP model. In Guided Inquiry, *inquiry process* refers to the stages of the ISP. These terms can be used interchangeably. The objective of Guided Inquiry is to provide assistance and instruction to guide students through the stages of the ISP, leading to competence in learning from a variety of sources of information.

From the students' perspective, inquiry is a search for meaning that is often fraught with misconceptions. Students frequently make the serious mistake of thinking that the main task in the inquiry process is to locate sources that relate to their topic, project, or problem. After selecting their topics, many students expect to be able to move directly to collecting information and presenting their findings. Unfortunately many instructional programs teach students about conducting research by actually describing the process in this way, neglecting the exploration and formulation essential for learning through inquiry. The most important task of the inquiry process is to explore information and ideas within sources and to form new understanding from these ideas. It is not unusual for students to be left to their own devices in this most challenging task of the inquiry process. All too often the result is blatant copying, narrow fact finding, and unimaginative repetition of an author's work, with little real learning on the part of the student.

The inquiry process is getting ideas to write about from new information. It is closely related to the writing process as described in Janet Emig's (1971) groundbreaking research. It is the prewriting stage of the writing process, when students are exploring and formulating ideas. Writing blocks are actually thinking blocks in which thoughts haven't been sufficiently formed to present ideas. The inquiry process precedes the writing process to prepare students for writing by giving them something to talk about and in turn write about. It is during the inquiry process that students build constructs for writing, composing, and creating.

Without forming a focus, the student is merely collecting unrelated facts. One high school student explained the problem in this way:

I had a general idea not a specific focus. As I was writing, I didn't know what my focus was. When I was finished, I didn't know what my focus was. My teacher says she doesn't know what my focus was. I don't think I ever acquired a focus. It was an impossible paper to write. I would just sit there and say, "I'm stuck." If I learned anything from that paper it is, you have to have a focus. You have to have something to center on. You can't just have a topic. You should have an idea when you start. I had a topic but I didn't know what I wanted to do with it. I figured that when I did my research it would focus in. But I didn't let it. I kept saying, "this is interesting and this is interesting and I'll just smush it all together." It didn't work out.

Rather than just "smushing it all together," Guided Inquiry enables students to formulate a focus as they work through the inquiry process. This focus is developed during the exploration and formulation stages under the guidance of the instructional team.

Another student explained that formulation requires reflection, time, and effort: "I've learned that this is the way it works. Tomorrow I'll read this over and some parts will fall into place and some still won't . . . . The mind doesn't take everything and put it into order automatically and that's it. Understanding that is the biggest help." Inquiry is hard work but well worth the effort. It involves not merely narrowing a topic but formulating a topic. The participants in these studies referred to this as forming an angle or strategy, a perspective or point of view, something that someone else might not have thought of in this way; a new way of looking at something.

Rather than claiming that inquiry is a simple matter of locating sources, Guided Inquiry provides explanation and intervention that supports students throughout the complex inquiry process. Through Guided Inquiry students come to a deeper knowledge of the subject and gain an understanding of their own inquiry process, as well as the basic skills and abilities to locate, evaluate, and use information for learning and presentation.

Vygotsky's Notion of Intervention

The concept of higher-order thinking, as explored and explained by Vygotsky (1978), is an important element of constructivist theory. The development of higher-order thinking is fostered by guidance in what he calls the zone of proximal development. "The zone of proximal development is the distance between the actual developmental level as determined by independent problem solving and the level of potential development as determined though problem solving under adult guidance or in collaboration with more capable peers" (1978, p. 131).

Building on Vygotsky's concept, we can think of teaching as organizing the learning environment so that students are confronted with questions drawn from their own experience and curiosity. Schools need to provide resources for students to explore questions, with guidance at critical points in the learning process. Borrowing from Vygotsky's concept of a zone of proximal development, we can develop guidance around a "zone of intervention, in which a student can do with advice and assistance what he or she cannot do alone or can do only with great difficulty" (Kuhlthau, 2004). Teachers and librarians who are able to recognize those critical moments when intervention and instruction are essential can tailor interventions to enable students to achieve understanding in the learning process.

The studies of the ISP indicate that the exploration and formulation stages are when higher order thinking is developed by carefully planned advice and assistance of the instructional team. In Guided Inquiry this is a zone of intervention when specific instruction and assistance is given to guide students to formulate their focus as a path for collecting information to complete their task. Unfortunately students frequently are left on their own during these critical but confusing stages of learning in research assignments.

Developing Basic Inquiry Abilities in Young Children

The Guided Inquiry approach is organized around the six stages of the ISP, developed in extensive study of the information-seeking process of middle and secondary students. The studies of teenagers offer a clear direction for engaging younger children in inquiry learning that will lay the foundation for competence as they grow.

This approach for elementary students has evolved from earlier work first presented in *School Librarian's Grade by Grade Activities Program* (Kuhlthau, 1981) but adapted for 21st-century schools and research on third space in elementary schools by Maniotes. It lays out the importance of merging students' outside-of-school worlds with the curriculum in schools to make learning meaningful, powerful, and relevant, and of Caspari's application of object-based learning in preschool and in the primary grades.

Guided Inquiry for young children seeks to incorporate the most natural ways children learn at early stages of cognitive development. Although the approach owes much to the Swiss psychologist Jean Piaget's concept of stages in cognitive growth, we recognize that a lock-step developmental approach is counterproductive. The concept of cognitive development makes it possible to plan inquiry activities that students can respond to and learn from. The young child, prior to age 7 and up to age 11, can perform mental operations on a concrete level. After age 12 most children can use abstract thought, generalize, and form a hypothesis. The ISP requires all three. That does not mean that the child under age 12 cannot be involved in inquiry. This is an ideal time to set the stage for engaging in the full inquiry experience, incorporating all stages of the inquiry process, from forming a focus perspective to presenting. There are abilities that children can learn and can draw from when they are ready to use more abstract assimilation of multiple sources to create a cohesive understanding, as described in the ISP model.

Many of the activities in *School Librarian's Grade by Grade Activities Program* engage children in four basic abilities in using information for learning: recall, summarize, paraphrase, and extend. The very youngest child can respond to a text or other information by recalling what he or she has seen or heard, summarizing by selecting certain facts or ideas, paraphrasing by retelling in his or her own words, and extending by adding something more that he or she already knows. These are basic skills that are essential in information seeking and use in the inquiry process in middle and secondary school. Young children prepare for complex inquiry projects by extensive practice in these basic inquiry abilities. Guided Inquiry builds these basic abilities in prekindergarten to fifth grade through an inquiry approach to learning.

Six Principles of Guided Inquiry

We have shown how Guided Inquiry is grounded in a constructivist approach to learning and is based on the research into students' perspectives on the ISP. Six fundamental concepts are drawn from this theoretical research base to form the underlying principles of Guided Inquiry (see Figure 2.4). These principles are based on what we know about how children learn, firmly grounded in the substantial work of Dewey, Bruner, Kelly, Vygotsky, and Piaget. Guided Inquiry adopts these concepts and adapts them for learning in 21st-century schools.

Children Learn by Being Actively Engaged in and Reflecting on an Experience

Engagement and reflection are two fundamental components of Guided Inquiry. As we have discussed, Dewey (1933) described learning as an active individual process that takes place through a combination of acting and reflecting on the consequences. Bruner's (1973) studies of perception and his later writings (1994) expanded on the constructivist view of the nature of human thinking and learning. Bruner's research confirmed that people learn best when they are actively involved in making sense of the world rather than passive receivers of information. He explained that it is not enough for people to merely gather information; they need to be involved in interpreting for deep understanding to occur. Learning involves "going beyond the information given" to create "products of mind."

The Six Principles of Guided Inquiry
Children learn by being actively engaged in and reflecting on an experience.
Children learn by building on what they already know.
Children develop higher-order thinking through guidance at critical points in the learning process.
Children have different ways and modes of learning.
Children learn through social interaction with others.
Children learn through instruction and experience in accord with their cognitive development.

Figure 2.4. Six Principles of Guided Inquiry.

Guided Inquiry is based on the premise that deep, lasting learning is a process of construction that requires students' engagement and reflection. An inquiry approach to learning seeks to motivate students to take ownership of their ideas and to create something that matters to them. Inquiry stimulates learning in students from the youngest age by engaging their innate curiosity, through middle childhood by enabling their quest for independence, and on into their teen years, when they are gaining a sense of self through their developing knowledge and expertise, which prepare them for the challenges of work and daily living in adulthood.

Motivation is an essential component of a constructivist approach to deep learning. Research on the ISP reveals that engagement and reflection are important in each stage of the inquiry process. Reflection and thinking about the ideas encountered in the inquiry process enable students to construct knowledge and meaning. However, engagement may falter, particularly in the exploration and formulation stages, when students are not expecting the conflict of ideas and information they encounter. Guided Inquiry is a program for helping students through the inquiry process, encouraging engagement and reflection in each stage of learning.

Children Learn by Building on What They Already Know

One of the basic tenets of constructivist theory is that past experience and prior understandings form the basis for constructing new knowledge. Major educational theorists have provided an extensive body of literature on how children build schema or constructs that form their view of the world. The central concept of these theorists is that connections to a child's present knowledge are essential for constructing new understanding.

In Guided Inquiry students build on what they already know to form a personal perspective on the world around them. They develop skills and abilities for successful living and contributing in the world. The process of construction is an active, ongoing process of learning that continues throughout life. Students are guided through inquiry by asking: What do I already know? What more do I want to know? How do I find out? What did I learn? How do I use what I learned? What will I do next time?

Studies reveal that students approach research that they generate themselves with more engagement than the research imposed upon them by a school assignment (Gross, 1998). McNally's (2005) study of research in secondary schools found that students who were able to select their own topics within a curriculum area were more engaged and successful than students given narrowly defined topics by the teacher. At the initiation stage of the ISP, when a research assignment is first announced, it may seem like an imposed task. An important component of Guided Inquiry and a challenge for the instructional team is to transform a school task into one that is self-generated by students, one that builds on what they already know.

Continuity between the curriculum within the school and the child's experiences outside the school promotes sustained, meaningful learning. Therefore, the curriculum and the student's world need to be closely aligned for deep personal learning to take place. Too often school learning seems removed and irrelevant to the student. In Guided Inquiry we use the concept of third space. Third space is a theoretical place in which students' outside experience is viewed in school as important and relevant to all learning (Maniotes, 2005). Often in schools the curriculum is the sole focus of learning. But when the students' understandings and experiences are called upon to make sense of the curriculum, a powerful learning environment is achieved. The child's world may be thought of as first space and the curriculum of the school as second space. Third space is where the two come together in a meaningful way and where deep learning takes place. When we consider all children as people who have rich lives outside the school context, we realize that there is a wide range of information they draw from to make sense of their world. Third space is an important component in Guided Inquiry, and will be discussed in more detail in Chapter 3.

Children Develop Higher-Order Thinking Through Guidance at Critical Points in the Learning Process

Unfortunately, most school work is limited to shallow processing in response to simple or superficial questions with prescribed answers. Deep processing requires engagement and motivation that stimulate inquiry within a constructivist approach to learning. Deep processing fosters higher order thinking, which requires intervention at critical points in the learning process.

Vygotsky's notion of a zone of proximal development is helpful in thinking of how and when to intervene in students' inquiry process. Vygotsky, a Soviet psychologist whose work had a profound influence on learning theory, developed the concept of identifying an area or a zone in which intervention would be most helpful to a learner. The zone of proximal development is the distance between actual developmental level as determined by independent problem solving and the level of potential development as determined through problem solving under professional guidance or in collaboration with more capable peers. This concept provides a way of understanding intervention in the constructive process of another person.

The zone of intervention in Guided Inquiry may be thought of as that area in which a student can do with advice and assistance what he or she cannot do alone or only with great difficulty. Intervention within this zone enables students to progress in the accomplishment of their tasks. Intervention outside this zone is inefficient and unnecessary, and may be experienced by students as intrusive on the one hand and overwhelming on the other.

As the ISP model shows, students often have difficulty in the early stages of the inquiry process. Even when they begin with great enthusiasm and initial success, many soon become confused and uncertain about how to proceed. This sense of uncertainty is an indication of a need for assistance and instruction, a zone of intervention. There are certain times in the inquiry process when students cannot move ahead or can move ahead only with great difficulty; these are the times when they are most in need of assistance and most open to instruction. At these times the instructional team has an opportunity to guide the inquiry for engaging, lasting, deep learning.

Students need intervention tailored to each stage of the inquiry process. Guided Inquiry offers guidance throughout the process that enables creative learning from a variety of sources of information. Intervention is carefully planned to develop higher order thinking from early grades through high school.

Guided Inquiry enhances learning by targeting specific areas of concern and providing intensive intervention at key points where instruction, guidance, and reflection are required. It employs flexible grouping, sometimes intervening with a whole class, at other times in small groups, and occasionally giving individual instruction and guidance.

Children Have Different Ways and Modes of Learning

Constructivist theory recognizes learning as a holistic experience incorporating many ways of knowing. Children learn through all their senses. They apply all their physical, mental, and social capabilities. The concept of multiple intelligences developed by Howard Gardner (1983) helps us to envision these many ways of learning, with students commonly excelling in one more than another. His theory includes linguistic, musical, logical-mathematical, spatial, bodily-kinesthetic, personal, and social intelligences. A wide range of resources in an array of formats presented through a variety of activities offers children a wealth of opportunities for learning. Reading, listening, viewing, and observing are joined with writing, speaking, performing, and producing to encompass the holistic experience of learning. Inquiry learning offers many ways to construct deep understandings of the world and one's life in it.

Technology has broadened the scope and variety of resources available for learning. The Internet provides vast access to digital materials. In this book we incorporate print texts available in the school library and digital texts available online with local museum objects and even digitized museum collections online. This combination of print and visual images and objects offers a wide range of media for accommodating different ways of knowing and learning.

The ISP models the stages in the process of learning from a variety of sources. Guided Inquiry is planned to provide many ways of generating ideas, including stories and narratives that foster images and imagination as well as use of expository texts for determining importance. The incorporation of museum collections further expands the resources for generating ideas and for promoting many ways of knowing and finding meaning. Products of inquiry take many forms, incorporating the whole range of multiple intelligences.

Children Learn Through Social Interaction with Others

Children are constantly learning through interaction with others around them. The experience of learning through interaction is called *social construction*. Children construct their understandings of the world through continuous, ongoing interaction with the people in their lives. Parents, peers, siblings, teachers, acquaintances, and strangers are all part of the social environment that forms a learning environment in which children are continuously constructing and making meaning for themselves.

Vygotsky describes a specific social nature and process by which children grow into the intellectual life of those around them. Kelly's theory includes a social corollary that stresses the importance of the social context in a person's process of construction. Bruner writes of the influence of social interaction in learning and knowledge construction. Dewey's progressive education created schools modeled on interaction in communities. All of these constructivist theorists recognized the importance of a dynamic social environment for relevant learning.

There is a delicate balance between learning through social interaction and constructing for oneself. Traditional research assignments were commonly done as independent work. Collaborating with classmates affords the opportunity to help students think things through. While we acknowledge the importance of collaborating, some group projects foster very little individual learning. Caution needs to be taken to ensure that group activity enables deep individual learning through social interaction. Guided Inquiry considers the students engaged in inquiry a community of learners. This community offers opportunities for interaction with others that promote learning and an audience for sharing what has been learned.

Children Learn Through Instruction and Experience in Accord with Their Cognitive Development

Constructivists recognize and respect cognitive development as an important consideration in learning. Piaget (Elkind, 1976) describes children as progressing through stages of cognitive development, with their capacity for abstract thinking increasing with age. The young thinker may have difficulty dealing with the more abstract aspects of inquiry. Since the inquiry process requires considerable abstraction, there is a need to accommodate inquiry tasks to the child's level of cognitive development. Although learning may not always occur in the exact stages identified by Piaget, we gain insight into the cognitive development of the child through his work.

Guided Inquiry is carefully planned, closely supervised, targeted intervention by an instructional team that leads children through inquiry learning from the early ages through their teen years, with the goal of developing deep understanding and independent learning. Bruner advocated introducing at an early age the ideas and styles that in later life make an educated person. He called for a "spiral curriculum" that respects the ways of thought of the growing child and translates material into logical forms that are challenging enough to tempt the child to advance (Bruner, 1977). Guided Inquiry is based on the idea of a spiral curriculum that challenges children to learn through inquiry compatible with their level of cognitive development.

Guided Inquiry is carefully designed for learning in each stage of cognitive development. In prekindergarten through fifth grade, inquiry learning involves children asking questions, seeking answers, and sharing their discoveries with others. Children in middle school are in a stage of transition to more abstraction in learning. These students explore ideas from various sources and integrate those ideas into their own thinking. They are preparing for forming a focused perspective within the process of information seeking that they can develop for sharing and applying. Secondary school students' learning centers on the inquiry process, building on the knowledge and strategies they have acquired throughout elementary and middle school. Through these years, as students' capacity for abstraction and independence increases, the Guided Inquiry team gradually releases responsibility to them in preparation for learning, living, and working in the information society.

Connecting to the Students' World

3

*I try to steer them toward something that will create a spark; toward books
they will make connections with, or things they will have questions about,
or ways they can use their own background knowledge.*
                                                            —fourth-grade teacher

As discussed in the last chapter, Guided Inquiry is based on current research, yet it is also grounded in the ideas of John Dewey. Both approaches agree that learning should be at the heart of schools. All students deserve an education that teaches them to acquire and use information to make informed decisions and intelligent choices and to continue to learn throughout their lives. It is time for educators to think of schools as learning communities. The Guided Inquiry approach is an alternative to the industrial age model and is based in learning.

Through Guided Inquiry students are able to incorporate what they have already learned with new information, come up with theories of their own, and investigate their world. Students learn how to find information pertinent to their investigations and how to synthesize that information to present it to others. Students learn to plan and make decisions throughout the inquiry process. These are important life skills in today's world, and they can be learned in schools.

In order for students to be able to create understandings of their own, educators must begin by listening to them. In this chapter we address the important Guided Inquiry concept of bringing the students' "outside of school" world and the curriculum together.

Building on Students' Questions

Harada and Yoshina describe learning through inquiry as "continuous, authentic, social, hands-on" (2004, p. x). A natural and authentic process, inquiry learning guided by an instructional team can be a powerful tool to help students connect what they know from outside of school to what they must learn in school. What do students know about the world? What are they interested in? Are there examples from their world that could help them explain the curriculum content of the class? How can we tap into those rich and varied experiences that they bring with them to school?

In an inquiry approach, the questions that students address in schools are their own. Educators often puzzle over how to motivate students to learn the curriculum. When the learning is driven by students' own questions and connects to their own understandings of the world, motivation is natural and intrinsic. Through this approach what students learn in school helps them to understand what they experience outside of school. And their outside experience is called upon to help them make sense of what they are learning in school.

When the achievement of standards is the only focus of the classroom, teachers often resort to the difficult task of finding ways to make disconnected objectives more palatable. However, when Guided Inquiry is at the heart of teaching and learning, there is no need to look elsewhere for motivation. Students are internally motivated when the majority of learning comes from their own real questions about curricular content. Guided Inquiry naturally incorporates students' own lives into the curriculum through their real questions and through what Dewey called an "organic connection" (1902, p. 201).

Wells (2000) describes a "real question" in two ways. First, it is a question the answer to which the teacher and students have a true desire to know. Second, it is one that students could take on and own by offering opinions based on the evidence from their own life experiences as well as the resources they find. Real questions create an organic environment of inquiry in which teachers and students come together because they honestly want to find out and learn.

Harste (1994) describes inquiry as an approach to learning in which teachers consider their classrooms as communities of learners, and the inquiry of students is at the center of the learning. Creating a classroom full of individuals who see themselves as a community of learners requires attention on the part of the instructional team. An open, receptive environment is key. The instructional team's philosophy on learning and how they interact with their students play a large role in the creation of that environment. When the central goal is the formation of new concepts through the process of inquiry, and students and teachers are willing to break out of traditional roles, a community of learners can be achieved. However, valuing students' input and ideas takes continual work in the art of teaching and listening that goes beyond the everyday norm. Finally, an inquiry approach in a community of learners allows teachers and students together to create "real questions," allowing ample room for students' own queries.

Maniotes (2005) studied students' conversations about literary texts to investigate the ways they draw on their outside experience for learning in school. The following example is from a discussion in a fourth-grade classroom in which the teacher had set up literature circles to discuss a variety of books they had read. This group of fourth graders had read *Superfudge* (Blume, 2003), and the character Fudge had just found out that his family was going to move. Isaac, one of the students, had moved quite often in his nine years. He asked the group, "How would you feel, if you were Fudge, about the move?" Through the students' answers to his real question, Isaac learned a lot about his peers and had multiple responses to think about when considering the character's feelings in the text (Maniotes, 2005, p. 133):

Sheila: If I was around Fudge's age I wouldn't remember 'cause he is so little . . . when I was little, I was living in Metro City and I had to move to Mountainveiw . . . . I feel a little strange . . . when I move from one place to another.

Isaac: Hermione? (Hermione is raising her hand.)

Hermione: I would feel sad because when I moved from Metro City to Mountainview, I lost my best friend Annie. She used to understand what I was going through and we used to talk about everything. And we used to play together and do everything together. And I just really miss her.

Isaac: My third one was, have you ever moved from one spot to another and moved back? Hermione?

Hermione: Yes, I have moved to places and then back. I moved to Oklahoma and then to Metro City . . . and then to Nevada and then I came back to Metro City and then I came to Mountainview.

Isaac: James?

James: Once, I moved to Texas for like a year or two, and then I came back to Mountainview and then I moved again and then I came back to Mountainview.

Isaac: Sheila?

Sheila: I moved. I kept on moving from Metro City to Mountainview when I was in third and second grade. For mostly second grade, I was staying in Mountainview and then I moved back to Metro City and then I moved back to Mountainview and then I finally stayed in Mountainview.

Isaac: I want to answer that too 'cause first we lived in Rosemont, then we moved to Texas for a year or two and then we moved back to Rosemont and then we moved to Metro City then to Mountainview.

Analysis of this conversation reveals how they drew from their outside experience to make sense of the text. Isaac began this conversation with a question related to understanding the character's feelings, because Fudge's reluctance to move resonated with him. This was a real question that related to Isaac's life and, as he found out, to the lives of several of the other students.

Sheila showed that she was interpreting the text and the character's feelings. She also drew on her own experiences to come up with a theory that Fudge wouldn't recall much about it because he was so little. Hermione also theorized that Fudge would be sad to miss his friends. Using their own life and cultural experiences, the students made sense of the text in answering Isaac's real questions. Through a question stemming from their own experience these students were able to interact with the text in an organic connection, to empathize with the character, Fudge, and to relate meaningfully to a theme in the literature.

Third Space: Merging Curriculum and Questions

The preceding dialogue is an example of third space interaction of personal experience and curriculum content. There are two types of student experience. One is the varied experience of the individual taken from life outside school, which may be thought of as the first space. The other is the curriculum content of the classroom, identified as the second space. It is important for educators to know how to help students use their cultural knowledge and experiences from everyday life to help them understand the curriculum content. When both come into play in equal amounts, that is the third space.

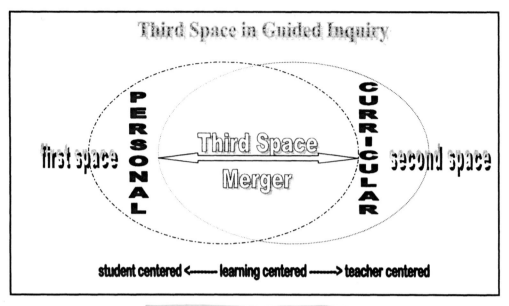

Figure 3.1. Third Space in Guided Inquiry.

Figure 3.1 represents the third space. The first space is the personal and cultural out-of-school knowledge and ways of knowing. The second space is the official curricular knowledge and school ways of knowing. The third space is where the two overlap and merge to create a new, hybrid form. Here students are flexibly and fluently using their outside knowledge to interpret, understand, and make sense of in-school curriculum, ideas, and ways of knowing. The broken lines represent a permeable boundary around the official and the personal ways of knowing, not fixed, but ever changing.

The notion of "third space" arises out of hybridity theory (Bhabha, 1994), which education researchers have found calls for reconceptualizing classrooms as hybrid spaces. A common use of the term *hybrid* refers to a car that will run on electricity or gas. But the use of *hybrid* in classrooms is more closely linked to hybrid roses. When two types of roses are mixed, they create an altogether new form. Peach-colored roses are a hybrid cross between yellow and pink. When we think of classrooms as hybrid spaces that use outside-of-school knowledge to make sense of the curriculum, inside school knowledge, we find that new ways of talking and learning occur in third space (Maniotes, 2005). This requires educators to pull away from the either/or of child-centered learning or curriculum-centered teaching. In schools this tension is more loaded than the scientific binary. Escaping from this binary has the potential to transform schools into reaching the third space. Within third space, students can construct new worldviews rather than having to take on the teacher's perspective or those mandated by the curriculum or textbooks.

The Students' World as First Space

There are many definitions of this type of first space knowledge. Gutierrez, Rymes, and Larson (1995) describe it as "unofficial" knowledge and define it as the local and cultural knowledge of students. In their study, the unofficial included popular cultural references and information of personal import. Moll and Greenberg (1990) described students' "funds of knowledge." They stated that, "by mobilizing funds of knowledge we can transform class-rooms into more advanced contexts for teaching and learning" (p. 344). In order to mobilize the funds of knowledge, we must first recognize them. Through an exploration of community and school learning, these researchers provided two examples in which children's literacy was used to mediate and analyze their interactions with the "living knowledge" brought to the classroom by social networks.

Moll and Greenberg described one example in which a classroom took on an inquiry ap-proach. The teacher chose the topic of building construction, knowing that many of the stu-dents' parents were in this type of work. The students used their literacy and research skills to find out about the history of construction. Later the parents came in to talk to the class as ex-perts on construction. The addition of community experts to the unit was found to "contrib-ute(d) substantively to the development of the lessons, to access their funds of knowledge for academic purposes. Theirs was an intellectual contribution to the content and process of classroom learning" (1990, p. 339).

What students bring to school with them in the way of knowledge about the world is com-plex. In an ethnography of Latino students over four years, Moje and her colleagues (2004) found that students' "funds of knowledge" are complex and multilevel, containing the four main categories of family, community, peer, and popular culture. Through their deep inspec-tion of the students' funds of knowledge as well as their schoolwork, the researchers found that the gap between the curriculum and students' out-of-school knowledge is not "as vast" as we often assume it to be (2004, p. 41). Thus, "what counts as valid or worthwhile knowledge" was more of an "epistemological distance" than a real difference between home and school infor-mation (p. 41). Still, when teachers see unofficial knowledge as unwelcome or unimportant to school learning, the distance expands. If teachers can tap into this knowledge that students bring with them, as in Guided Inquiry, the effect can be quite powerful.

The Curriculum as Second Space

At times teachers get bogged down by mandated district and national curriculum goals that hinge on designated standards and testing dates. While goals and standards can constrain, they can also be helpful gifts for teaching. We discuss in chapter 7 how the curriculum lends it-self to this Guided Inquiry approach.

When overused, official or second space that is focused on learning curriculum in isola-tion can be a great detriment to students and can stifle the many perspectives of a class full of people with different experiences (Mehan, 1979; Moje, Ciechanowski, and Athan, 2001; Tay-lor and Dorsey-Gaines, 1988). Consider what is called the IRE sequence (O'Connor and Mi-chaels, 1996), common in traditional classrooms. When researchers looked at the talk in classrooms, they found a pattern of initiate, response, and evaluate (IRE). The teacher initiates a topic, the student responds to that question, and the teacher then evaluates that response. In this type of talk the teacher controls the discourse as well as the topic, and a very limited amount of student talk takes place. Some have described this as "official discourse." Rather than taking on a conversational tone in classrooms, teachers often use this official mode of communication. The problem with using such discourse is that it restricts the amount and quality of student input.

Gutierrez, Rymes, and Larson (1995) provided an excellent example. In their study of a ninth-grade social studies classroom, the majority of class time was spent in the monologic, of-ficial spaces where the teacher was in control of the discourse, the curriculum, and the learning.

In this "traditional" classroom, the official discourse regularly displaced the local and cultural knowledge of the students. Only one view was represented, consisting of the "correct" and predetermined answers to questions about the content of the lessons. Within such an environment, that monologic discourse stifled conversation and a critical stance.

Remaining in the monologic does not always mean that the teacher is the only one talking. Even when the students are involved, their contributions are often reiterations of information and facts that remain in the worldview of the teacher as the students "fill in the blanks." While it is important for students to know facts and terms, using monologic space is not appropriate for all, or even a majority, of learning. Students often lose interest, as the content seems to have little relation to their lives outside the classroom.

It is critical to see discourse as context dependent (Gee, 2000) and imbedded with ideologies. As Gee (1992) explains, stable patterns of discourse become socially accepted. Members learn which discourses are valued and not valued by that community. In schools, students quickly learn that the discourses that stem from their local and cultural knowledge are not valued in the traditional official spaces of the classroom. And this realization can lead to a variety of role choices. Students can choose to pay attention and contribute to the official discourse in explicitly predetermined ways, taking an interest in learning to appropriate the ideal student role. On the other hand, they can act as if they are participating, for feigning interest is a common student achievement. Or they can "act out," pushing against the boundaries of official discourse, though the result is often negative for the student.

Though students become experts at what is required and expected of them within the boundaries of the classroom, what happens when they need to take what is learned in school and use it in the reality of their lives? We can meet our students in the middle or third space and help them to make connections between curricular goals and their lived experiences. Let's consider an alternative to a traditional model.

Creating Third Space

Consider a class in which the students' input is as important as the curriculum in the teacher's eyes. Consider a classroom in which students' contributions are more numerous than the teacher's. Consider a class in which talk sounds more like a conversation. Consider a space in which the knowledge that students have from the outside world consistently joins together with the curricular content, helping them to inform their own worldviews. In Maniotes's (2005) research into students' conversations about literary text, she found considerable evidence of third space. Following is an example of what third space can look like and accomplish.

This example of third space is from a fourth-grade book club discussion about *The Lion, the Witch and the Wardrobe* (Lewis, 1950). It began with a real question and moved into the negotiation and joint construction of ideas as well as critique (Maniotes, 2005):

Marisol: Would you believe if someone told you there was a different country in a wardrobe?

Isabel: I wouldn't. But if I did go in there, I would. But I wouldn't say what Peter, Susan, and Edmund said, "You can't keep telling a lie, get over it!"

Pam: I KNOW. I thought that was kind of rude.

Isabel: Yeah.

Marisol: I would just kind of go in to see, 'cause it's kind of like fiction to say that there is another country in a wardrobe and . . .

Isabel: But if you actually saw it?

Pam: Yea. You'll believe it!

In conversation, many perspectives come out. This stretch of talk originated with Marisol's real question aimed at how the characters felt when they did not believe their sister's claim that Narnia was in the wardrobe. Marisol is questioning the very premise of the fantasy text here as well. The conversation is marked with joint construction as the girls add substantively to one another's ideas. Mercer (2000) calls this "interthinking," which he defines as the "joint, coordinated intellectual activity which people regularly accomplish using language" (p. 16). Isabel critiqued the character's actions and entered the role of the character by improvising about what they might have said in her own terms with, "Get over it!" Pam agreed with Isabel and added the categorization of their behavior as rude, and Isabel concurred.

Knowing the improbability of there being another land in the closet, Marisol agreed with Isabel that she too would have gone in to see for herself. Isabel then pushed Marisol's idea a bit further when she asked her question, implying that seeing is believing. This bit of dialogue shows these students engaged in conversation, adding to one another's ideas and listening carefully to what each other had to say. Not only do they get the essence of what happened in the book, they are able to imagine themselves in the story even to the point of talking like one of the characters, as well as critiquing the characters' actions by replacing them with their own hypothetical actions.

Through a real conversation, these students were able to investigate their own questions about the text that they were reading on their own terms. Their understanding of their world entered deeply into their making sense of the text, including their own interpretations. Through this conversation they are accomplishing many literacy goals, by using their own voices in third space. You may have noticed that the teacher was not even present in this sequence, and yet the students used vocabulary that stemmed from formal or official ways of knowing (it's like fiction) as well as personal ways of knowing (get over it!) to get to the bottom of the real question that Marisol posed. As you can see, in the third space students can accomplish more in classrooms, but they must be able to have their voices heard.

Establishing a Community of Learners

To create third space it is necessary to develop a community of learners who feel free to exchange their ideas with the teacher and one another (see Figure 3.2, p. 38). How do we help students to feel comfortable sharing their outside lives in the school setting? This is not as easy as it sounds. In schools we often use language that is limited to a specific kind of teacher talk and does not easily transfer to the outside world. Because of the structured setting of the classroom, often students do not feel it is appropriate to bring in these external ways of knowing, and they are often discouraged from doing so.

Establishing a Community of Learners

- Model personal connections
- Create a safe atmosphere
- Encourage students to speak freely
- Accept varied points of view
- Listen to ideas
- Consider students' ideas carefully

Figure 3.2. Establishing a Community of Learners.

Encouraging students to speak freely is one way we can help them feel comfortable. Another is to build our classes as a community of learners, in which there are many and various ways of talking and many and various experiences to draw from. As students see themselves as intellectual beings, and that their ideas and outside knowledge are valued, they can begin to be more comfortable volunteering in such a way in the school setting.

Establishing the class as a community of learners takes work. Teachers often consider this a project at the beginning of the year and, after a few weeks, decide the work is done, but this is a continuing and yearlong effort. Some issues to consider are what the objective in doing this is, what types of student groupings will be used, whether students are learning from each other, how the teacher should model for students by sharing outside experiences in school, how the teacher should respond to students' input, and how much students are talking compared to how much the teacher is talking.

Advantages of Small, Flexible Groups

Inquiry learning is a social process in which students learn from each other in a community of learners. Students need many opportunities to collaborate. Small, flexible groups provide students with opportunities to collaborate with others and share the many perspectives that they bring. Using small, interest-based groups through the inquiry process allows students to co-construct knowledge while collaborating on projects. Small groups also give students opportunities to learn from the varied sources they are working with. (See Figure 3.3.)

Advantages of Small, Flexible Groups

- More opportunities for student talk
- Close collaboration among peers
- Students learning from one another
- Opportunities for individual assessment of learning

Figure 3.3. Advantages of Small, Flexible Groups.

Whole class instruction cannot accomplish this intricate social collaboration, because students need many opportunities to try out their ideas. Small groups provide each student with many more opportunities to have a turn at talking and sharing. In these small groups the instructional team can interact with each student through interviewing, conferences, and assessment for intervention.

Creating a community of learners requires an instructional team to think through what they are asking students to do that promotes learning and collaboration throughout the inquiry process. The community of learners provides opportunities for students to work in the third space and bring together their outside interests, experiences, and knowledge with the content of the curriculum in the context of the school, creating an engaging forum for Guided Inquiry.

We can consider creating a community of learners for learning in third space on both macro and micro levels. At the macro level, decisions are about curriculum and how subjects are to be taught. The micro level considers the actual conversations in the classroom and specific decisions about interactions.

Planning for Third Space in Guided Inquiry

On the macro level are decisions about how to teach subject matter, in what sequence, and through what methods. Each of these decisions on the part of the instructional team affects whether students feel part of a community. Some considerations for planning at the macro level are how much lecturing and discussion will occur, who will lead the discussion, how students will be assessed, whether portfolio and conferences will be used to track student learning, and whether students will work in groups or as a whole class. These considerations determine how much students will be included in the learning process and the degree to which third space will be created.

Embedded in Guided Inquiry are Kuhlthau's (2004) Six Cs. These are important to the inquiry process and are key methods for creating a community of learners. The Six Cs—collaborate, converse, continue, choose, chart, and compose—are useful strategies when an instructional team works toward creating a learning community. They are discussed in detail in chapter 9.

Conversations and discussions are an important part of making students feel at home in the classroom community. Through opportunities to collaborate, students will converse. Thinking and talking are very closely connected, and when students have opportunities to converse they are able to think together in the co-construction of new knowledge. Helping young children recall, paraphrase, summarize, and extend their knowledge through conversations is a key element in the inquiry process. At the macro level the instructional team provides the students with many and varied opportunities to have conversations.

Conversing with the members of the instructional team also has benefits. As we explore in depth in chapter 9, the Guided Inquiry approach incorporates teacher–student conferences to check in on learning and guide students through the inquiry process. Conversations play a major role in a community of learners.

Also at the macro level, the instructional team provides opportunities to nurture learning by supporting it over time. Continuing learning through an extended inquiry project and helping students to do so is an important objective of Guided Inquiry. In a community of learners students have multiple opportunities and time to reflect on what they have learned. When time to reflect on learning is in the regular schedule, it shows students a commitment to thinking, learning, and having big ideas. Providing time for reflection in class helps to establish the community of learners, where value is placed on student learning. Also important to continuing a project is providing opportunities for students to make connections between information gathered and known and to plan ways to share what they have learned. Heath, Boehncke, and Wolf (2005) report the urgent need for students to have multiple opportunities to talk. Through making plans and sharing ideas with adults working as facilitators in project development, young people increase their language use and repertoire.

Another macro level decision is the amount of choice students have in the inquiry process. Decisions related to choice include how to offer choice in the assignment, how to provide for learning to choose what is important from texts, how to encourage choosing various formats to move thinking forward, and how to develop the creation of charts for visual thinking.

Composing in journals takes place throughout the Guided Inquiry process. Journals provide a forum for getting ideas down and connecting them to new information. They also provide a way of communicating feelings through the inquiry process so that the instructional team may intervene with assistance and instruction at the right moments. Journals help students organize their thoughts and provide a jumping-off point for focused conversations about their projects. Techniques such as summaries, two-column note taking, and sticky notes are other forms of writing that help students to communicate and organize throughout the inquiry process.

Strategies for Creating Third Space

Strategies for creating third space can be considered at the conversational level. This section discusses the details of conversations to consider the role of teacher talk in the creation of a community of learners. In an in-depth case study of one teacher, who was able to generate authentic academic conversations regularly, Maniotes (2005) found that the teacher consistently used three strategies to encourage students' input: modeling, conversing, and listening. Creating a community of learners at all grade levels requires that teachers model their own thinking, encourage students in support of conversations, and listen to students with an ear to making connections to the curriculum. A close examination of this teacher through many classroom discussions and conversations offers a useful example for micro level planning. Because we don't often think about how the subtle nuances of our speech affect our students' ways of responding, it is important to consider some specifics here. Each strategy is discussed in detail to consider the important role of the teacher's talk.

Modeling

Modeling is a powerful tool used to gently guide students in the direction the teacher wants them to go. As Gallas (1995) explained, establishing an "I wonder" context helps children get into a "let's find out" mode. The instructional team sets this "I wonder" mode by being open to their own puzzlement and wonderings as well as that of the students. In Guided Inquiry, questioning is shared by all members of the learning community. Teachers modeling their own questions helps students get into the "I wonder" mode.

In Maniotes's (2005) research the teacher, rather than giving students a direction to do something, often just showed them how. She modeled ways that helped students focus on the text when that was needed. She also modeled how to share her own personal responses, showing the students that this was not only all right to do, it was expected of them.

The teacher modeled all kinds of behaviors and talk through these conversations. She modeled how to think about a text, including backing up arguments, using cross-textual references, integrating new vocabulary into ideas, using what one already knows to make sense of new information, demonstrating how to do a specific task, and thinking in meta-cognitive ways.

Rather than tell the students that they should include their own personal connections, she modeled this for them. Forty percent of her modeling highlighted her own personal contributions. For example, the teacher modeled real-world book club behavior, "That's what I am going to do in my book club tomorrow, talk about what we should read next." In addition, she shared stories about her own childhood, "Yea, I used to feel that way about my brothers too. Even though they annoyed me, when they weren't there I missed them, even though I knew that if they were there, they probably would be bugging me" (2005, p. 220). Using modeling in many forms was a very useful tool to show students how to have a conversation as a community of learners.

Encouraging

Acknowledging and giving credit to students for making appropriate remarks or bringing personal knowledge into the school setting is another important role the teacher plays. Almost one-quarter of the teacher's comments were remarks encouraging students when they were headed down the right path. Focusing on the positive things students were doing was a useful conversational tool that the teacher used over and over again. The teacher's praise for her students came often and in many forms (Maniotes, 2005):

- "Neat! That's pretty cool. So in a way she's lucky. She's got a lot going for her . . . ."

- "That was a really good point, and I was going to ask the same question."

- "Good way to say it, Bud!"

- "I am so impressed that you picked up on that."

- "I also really enjoyed how he shared his connections from his own life."

In these examples the teacher is praising both academic ways of talking and sharing connections from outside with the other members of the community of learners. Sharing personal information can build trust, and of course it takes trust to share such information. Encouragement from the teacher to share these types of things and a positive reception to sharing personal information has a considerable impact on the learning community environment.

The teacher made it a point to encourage the students to talk. Rather than taking control and making evaluative statements, which tend to stop the conversation, the teacher had a way of inviting students back into the conversation. Following is an example.

In this class a student, Isabel, was moved by the *The Watsons Go to Birmingham—1963* to describe her father's racism. In this segment she described a time when her father got into trouble at school for making racist comments (2005, p. 224):

Isabel: Yea, like my dad. He got busted for it. In school, because he went to school in Florida, and there was a lot of people from like the country . . . and all those places. And he got in trouble. And he had detention for like two days or a week or something.

Teacher: Yea, it's just not the right thing to do, is it? So it kind of makes you rethink the whole idea of using those words.

Isabel: He told me that, as a lesson to learn.

Teacher: As a lesson to learn?

Isabel: Learn from other people's mistakes.

Teacher: Good! I'm glad that he can teach you that. That's pretty brave of him to admit that he makes mistakes, huh?

Isabel: He made a ton of mistakes.

The teacher used this technique repeatedly during the conversation. She first said, "It's just not the right thing to do, is it?" The question "is it" at the end opened the dialogue back up to Isabel after the teacher made an evaluative statement about Isabel's story. Later, she used an involvement-promoting "huh?" at the end of her statement to draw Isabel back into the conversation once more. The teacher made another evaluative statement, this time positive, and then provided Isabel a way back into the conversation. If the teacher did not use the "huh?" at the end of her conversational turn, it could have seemed as if she were evaluating Isabel's father in order to conclude the discussion. But instead, the teacher consistently opened the conversation back up to the students rather than having the final say.

Encouraging students to support one another through conversation is more important than you may think to get students to see themselves as a community of learners. Another essential aspect is listening.

Listening

There are many ways that teachers can show students that they are listening. Eye contact while they are speaking and overt listening behaviors are important. Also important are the statements that the teacher makes following students' comments. Many conversational moves can show that you are listening, such as repeating students' words, clarifying the content, paraphrasing, summarizing, and synthesizing. These all make you look like a careful listener. However, there have been studies showing that when teachers do these things, they must do so cautiously or they may give the wrong message.

As Maybin concludes, when teachers repeat and reformulate students' ideas as through paraphrasing, "it could be argued that the discourse . . . is monologic rather than dialogic. There is in effect only one voice speaking" (1999, p. 467). By rewording what the student says, the teacher can seem to be controlling the conversation by taking the words and changing them. Such paraphrasing or rewording can show a devaluing of students' own ideas. This would work against all efforts to create a community of learners. However, it depends on how you word your response. Consider the following example.

The way that the teacher worded her paraphrasings in the Maniotes study has a different feel. Her statements were, "Yea, so . . . ," "Ah, so . . . ," or "Oh, so . . . ." These kinds of constructions have the feel of emphasizing what someone said while simultaneously clarifying the meaning.

Following is a conversation from Maniotes's (2005) study of a group of fourth graders discussing the book *Because of Winn Dixie* (DiCamillo, 2000).

Isaac: Um. Gloria Dump she she said that that's um. those "That's where I keep all my ghosts um of my bad things." And Opal said, "You did all those bad things?" But she said, "No I did more."

Teacher: Say that part again.

Isaac: She said um. Opal asked if she did all um. each thing in the bottle. And Gloria Dump said that um. I've done more.

Teacher: Oh. So the bottles don't represent ALL the bad things she's done? Interesting. Anybody want to add to that?

Isaac: I want to add!

As you can tell by Isaac's hedging in the first line, he is having trouble explaining his point. First the teacher requests that he say it again, as his hedging has obscured his idea. By the end of his second turn, he has explained the conversation between Opal and Gloria, when Gloria confessed that she has done even more regretted acts than are represented by all the bottles on the tree. The teacher recognized that this was Isaac's point and reworded his response, showing that she understood his meaning.

Her "Oh so" construction showed him that she was trying to get the gist of what he was saying. Her paraphrasing also worked to simplify Isaac's response for the group. Through this act of paraphrasing, the teacher showed Isaac that she was listening and understood what he was working so hard to convey. The praise, "interesting," after her rewording shows that the teacher agrees with this idea and values his response. Then her final question bounces the conversation back to the group, and at the end of the segment Isaac jumps at the chance to add more.

The teacher's construction gave the students' words more power and clarity. As Maybin suggests, it is usually the teacher's voice that is highlighted through reformulation of thought. Yet in the case presented above, it was *clearly* the students' voices that were brought to the fore. Therefore, instead of guiding their voices to imitate her own or to reflect the official space of the classroom, as Maybin describes, this teacher's paraphrasing had an altogether different effect. Her constructions emphasized the students' voices in the classroom. By holding up students' ideas, the teacher effectively encouraged the conversations by careful listening.

Being an effective facilitator of discussions is an art that even an expert teacher has to work at. The previous examples show that creating a community of learners takes hard work at the micro level in the classroom. But with careful attention to honoring students' questions, taking time to let musing lead to connections, modeling, listening, and encouraging students in conversations, teachers can establish a solid community in which members learn from one another in third space.

Once the class is established as a community, many things can be accomplished through Guided Inquiry. Within that community, students are naturally motivated to answer their own authentic questions and discover new information. Guided Inquiry begins with valuing students' out-of-school knowledge.

Learning from Informational Texts

Although the examples of third space from Maniotes's research are of elementary school students investigating literature, they provide insight into developing third space that applies to all kinds of reading, viewing, and listening. Information literacy is closely allied to the traditional literacy of reading and reading comprehension, particularly of informational texts, expository texts, or nonfiction. (In this book the terms *informational texts, expository texts,* and *nonfiction* are used interchangeably.) Guided Inquiry employs the powerful combination of both literary and expository texts. The nature of inquiry is grounded in finding information, so informational texts are central to the task. However, literature in a variety of media can make the curriculum context come alive for students. For example, reading a vivid historical fictional account of an event at the beginning of the inquiry process draws students in, builds a common background, and sets the stage for the inquiry unit.

Many students need assistance in getting meaning out of expository texts. A recent source identified a common problem in reading informational material:

To the casual observer these kids were reading well. They chose books effortlessly. They read and shared in conferences and during sharing times. They were enthusiastic about the novels they read, and yet, when they read texts the teacher had chosen to set the stage for social studies and science learning, we watched many struggle to understand and then discuss what they read. Most were competent oral readers. They pronounced words correctly, missed few words, and sounded out words they didn't know. But many were so disconnected from the meaning of the text, especially expository text, that they were often unaware of the essence of what they were reading. (Keene and Zimmerman, 1997)

One teacher observed that, "These kids are fluent readers and many of them really like to read, but it's as if this fog bank rolls in when they're hit with challenging nonfiction" (Keene and Zimmerman, 1997, p. 83). This problem is common at all stages of reading development. Students need guidance in how to make connections between informational texts and what they already know. Guided Inquiry provides opportunities for students to discuss in third space the meaning and importance of expository texts.

Through Guided Inquiry the instructional team helps students to overcome the feeling of being unconnected with informational text. Through the inquiry process, students learn to "choose" what is important or pertinent to their question. Keene and Zimmerman call this determining importance in texts. In the interventions of Guided Inquiry, described in Chapter 9, the instructional team guides students to address their questions by choosing pertinent information and sharing their learning and forming new questions in a community of learners throughout the inquiry process. Thus, by the very nature of the process students are learning this essential literacy skill under the guidance of the instructional team.

Inquiry Circles: Learning in Small Groups

The students in the Maniotes study who were found to engage in third space were working in literature circles. The teacher employed an interpretation of literature circles described by Harvey Daniels (1994). Literature circles provide small groups of students with structure as a springboard for conversations. The structure is in place to help conversations grow out of the work they do independently on a common text. This is an excellent model for creating an environment in which students are responsible for independent learning through a guided approach. The teacher moves students toward independence by assigning them jobs to keep them focused. Each time the students meet, the jobs are rotated within the group. Gradually, as students learn what is acceptable in a literature circle they are able to do this on their own and need less structure.

This is an excellent model for small group instruction using nonfiction texts as well. In Guided Inquiry these are called inquiry circles. Students working in the same area of an inquiry unit are grouped together. During each Guided Inquiry session students work independently on tasks that prepare them for group discussion of the topic at hand. Daniels (1994) calls these tasks jobs. Each member of the circle has a specific job to do before the meeting.

While learning how to participate in literature circles, each student in the group takes on a different job. The idea is that each student learns how to do each of the jobs, being responsible for only one at a time until all are proficient at each task. Jobs are rotated to give students an opportunity to practice each type of task independently. In inquiry circles each task represents one aspect of inquiry that students need to learn. Prior to an inquiry circle students prepare for their parts. When the group comes together, they have a host of ways to look at one text or source of information.

Inquiry Circle Jobs	
Title	**Tasks**
WORD HUNTER	Finds key words and definitions
EVALUATOR	Evaluates the source
MESSENGER	Summarizes big ideas and main points
QUIZ KID	Raises questions
CONNECTOR	Makes connections between self, texts, and the world
NOTE TAKER	Takes specific notes on content
IMAGE MAKER	Creates a visual scheme of the ideas (flow chart, graphic organizer, drawing)
INTERPRETER	Asks, "What does it mean?" and "Why is it important?"

Figure 3.4. Inquiry Circle Jobs.

In preparation for the inquiry circle discussion, students record their work for their job in a section of their inquiry journals. Each student also records the citation of the source of information at the top of the journal page. The word hunter finds key words to share with the group. The evaluator judges the value of the source. The messenger looks for important ideas and major points for discussion. The quiz kid creates questions for the group to consider. The connector finds connections with other sources and with what he or she already knows. The note taker makes notes on specific details. The image maker makes drawings and charts of ideas found in the information source. The interpreter considers the larger issues of why this information is important and relevant to the topic. Other jobs may emerge as the inquiry proceeds, tailored to particular projects and age levels.

Once students are proficient at each job they can take on more than one job to prepare for a group meeting. For example, in the Maniotes study, as students felt more and more comfortable with the tasks, they took them on themselves. Once they learned the jobs, the students looked at each text with all eyes open and completed four or five of the jobs for one reading or group meeting. This is ideal and makes for the most engaging and interesting conversation. When each person has a different job the group meeting can tend to be like a round robin rather than a conversation.

It is important to strive for a conversation. When students understand the procedures and jobs they can critique one another and go back and forth. For example, they may have found the same information in more than one source and can share that in the inquiry circle. Or perhaps they have found conflicting information that prompts them to go back and examine the sources more deeply. If students are all doing different tasks, it is less likely that these comparisons will arise. It is important for students to engage each other during these meetings. Performing multiple jobs in preparation for the meeting helps students to interact in richer conversations.

It took considerable effort for the teacher in the Maniotes study to get students to that independent and self-motivated point in literature circles. There were many times when the teacher had to remind them that it was very important to have this work done before the group met. If a student did not complete the work, the group didn't have all the information they needed, and the discussion fell short of the students' expectations. Getting students to understand the reason for this independent work becomes easier as they discover the great conversations and collaboration they can have when all jobs are thoroughly completed before the meeting.

Another benefit of inquiry circles for teachers is that they provide an efficient context to plan for assessment. In Guided Inquiry, inquiry circles are set each week around independent work time. The group decides on the meeting dates as a deadline for their independent work. Instructional teams plan to step into groups and listen, taking assessment notes while the group is meeting. The team schedules individual conferences when the students are working independently in preparation for group meetings. Structurally, inquiry circles fit well into the Guided Inquiry approach and help the instructional team intervene with groups and individuals and assess students while they are working.

Inquiry circles differ from literature circles in that there are many forms the groups can take. In literature circles the students are all working around the same text. Inquiry circles can be accomplished in many different ways. The students might all be reading the same texts or using the same source. In this scenario each student in the group would perform a different task with that same source, approaching it from many angles. Having all the students examine one source provides a rich context for discussion, critique, and synthesis of the information. In another scenario the students work at a similar aspect of the inquiry, but using different sources. Reading level, number of texts available, computer time available, student interest, and varying independence with group work, among other student concerns, may all come into play as the instructional team decides what is best for their students at any given time. These two scenarios are just some of the possibilities. Students could work in pairs, or at times a circle may be composed of different aspects of the inquiry to consolidate information and learn from one another. Just as the structure of the groups may vary, the jobs also may vary depending on what the instructional team sees that students need. Jobs are in place to teach students the expectations for the learning as well as how to do the tasks required of that particular inquiry. The instructional team can take on inquiry circles with a flexible approach as they examine their students' learning needs.

A model like inquiry circles, in which students have specific jobs leading them to a conversation around these tasks, helps groups know what is expected and provides a context for richer and more involved discussions. Arranging inquiry circles in this way ultimately leads to synthesis of ideas, a main objective of Guided Inquiry.

Staying on Task

The Maniotes (2005) study recognized the delicate balance of student talk and curriculum in third space. Maniotes found that third space fell across a range of responses. There was third space emphasizing the personal, third space emphasizing the curriculum, and third space that fell in the middle, where the students' ideas and the curriculum were very well balanced. Each was drawing from the other to form richer understandings.

Student talk that is unrelated to the content of the curriculum may be unproductive for certain goals of learning. However, it may be essential for this talk to occur occasionally to promote social learning. Social talk can work to build trust and a level of comfort that students need in order to make comments about their personal lives. As mentioned earlier, context has everything to do with what people are willing to bring to a conversation.

A community of learners provides a context for third space with a high level of trust in all members. If the conversation is always in the teacher's control, students don't have an opportunity to use their own constructs about the world to help them understand the course content. This balance is tricky, but achievable. The hardest part for the instructional team is first allowing students to bring in outside information. The instructional team creates a setting in which students are comfortable contributing in real and natural ways.

Often the concern arises that students might get off track. This is why Guided Inquiry is essential. Students must be guided into knowing what is expected. The instructional team helps students draw the line and know what is acceptable in conversations. Students learn how to offer personal examples in relation to learning in appropriate ways, within a wide range of contexts. Often this type of intellectual conversation is not within students' experience. The instructional team guides students toward this balance by helping them make connections between outside information and curricular content. By making links accessible and prominent in conversation, the instructional team models how to stay on track. Modeling and listening to students are important aspects of this learning as well as a commitment to interactive conversation in classrooms. Guided Inquiry strives for a balance of third space, which takes continual commitment and effort.

Guided Inquiry: An Alternative for All Students

In Kozol's *The Shame of the Nation* (2005) he lays out the great disparities in American education today. It appears that there is a grand opportunity for Guided Inquiry to reshape schools. Kozol describes how schools in the neediest and poorest populations return again and again to the scientific model of teaching, which stems from the industrial age, of training students as laborers. Students are being limited by the very nature of the courses offered and approaches to education taken in these schools. Rather than looking at students with different potential as they come to school, schools are training them to work in the bottom segments of the workforce. All our children deserve opportunities to reach their fullest potential, and we can make this happen.

An alternative approach to the industrial age model, an inquiry approach based in learning, provides students with opportunities to maneuver in the complex world of information in which we live. With these inquiry skills under their control, students have many opportunities to reach their fullest potential in their understanding of the world and in their future work, whatever type of work that might be. A Guided Inquiry approach offers this alternative.

Throughout this chapter we have mentioned the importance of the instructional team. The following chapter discusses who the members of the instructional team are, and what their roles are in the Guided Inquiry process.

The Guided Inquiry Team

Everyone was doing the part he or she can do best. No one of us could do this alone.
—middle school reading teacher

Twenty-first-century schools call for rethinking how the learning environment is organized to prepare students for the global information society. For the most part, 20th-century schools were organized on a fixed model of one teacher with a class of 25 or more students. These schools were designed to prepare students for a localized, industrial society. Elementary school children were assigned to a single teacher, who taught all subjects with little outside involvement or enrichment. Middle and secondary students were assigned to lock-step subject area classes, meeting with each teacher at the same hour each day. Resources were mainly within the classroom, with school libraries providing collections of materials that varied in quality and quantity from school to school.

In too many instances this rigid structure of school staff and inflexible organization of the school day continues into the first decade of the 21st century. Too often school is unrelated to students' real-world experiences. The old model does not lend itself readily to an inquiry approach to learning or take full advantage of the varied experience of the educational staff of the school. The old model does not make good use of the resources available outside the school in the local community or the vast resources available in information technology. The old model does not adequately prepare students for independent learning in an information-rich environment, which is essential for living and working in the information age.

The global information technology of the 21st century requires students to be able to adapt, contribute, and thrive in a rapidly changing world. To prepare students for living and working in this environment an instructional team guides them through a constructivist approach to learning in the inquiry process. While you read this chapter, think about the instructional climate provided for the students in your school. Is your school organized to provide students with the ability to learn from a variety of sources of information in the 21st-century information environment? Does your school take full advantage of the varied expertise and specialization inside the school and in the outside community? Does your school provide a climate for collaboration and team instruction?

Taking Advantage of Expertise in the School

A flexible team approach to teaching is essential for addressing current needs and for implementing Guided Inquiry. A flexible model for the information age school incorporates a constructivist approach to learning with an environment for creating "third space," in which the curriculum meets the students' world in dynamic, interactive, deep learning. In Guided Inquiry, a core team plans the inquiry, but an extended team is necessary for success. The extended team may not work on the inquiry throughout, but rather enter when the core team feels they are needed. Administrators, teachers, and librarians all play important roles in making Guided Inquiry work. The teams include alliances outside the school with community partners in public libraries, museums, and other institutions. Each member of a team is a specialist, offering his or her unique expertise to meet the specific needs of students in a particular unit of study.

Team teaching is not a new idea in education, but it needs considerable revision to be effective for implementing Guided Inquiry. The main purpose of teaming in Guided Inquiry is to take full advantage of the varied expertise of the school faculty to provide optimal learning opportunities for students. Guided Inquiry mobilizes teachers and librarians into flexible instructional teams to collaborate in planning and implementing inquiry learning, bringing all of their special expertise to meet subject area curriculum objectives and information literacy goals as well as meeting the specific learning needs of the students. Flexibility is important in organizing teams to take full advantage of the varied expertise and knowledge of the members of the school staff to enhance student learning

Three-Member Instructional Teams

Although two-member collaborations, between one librarian and one teacher, are commonly used, three-member instructional teams are highly desirable for the most productive collaborative planning and teaching. Three people working together to design and guide inquiry offer a synergy for sharing ideas and creatively planning and solving problems. These three people form the core Guided Inquiry team. Important work on inquiry teams suggests that three-member teams function best for gaining the full advantage of collaboration. A basic instructional team is a subject area teacher and the school librarian. The third member joining the team may be a second classroom or subject area teacher or any of the other specialists in the school. There may be times when you are able to collaborate successfully with more than three people. However, too many subject areas with diverse objectives may merely clutter and confuse the inquiry, actually obstructing rather than enhancing learning. More is not necessarily better in Guided Inquiry.

Instructional teams may be made up from any combination of the whole range of experts inside the school, including subject specialists, reading specialists, learning abilities specialists, technology specialists, and music, art, and drama teachers. While each member of the instructional team has a particular specialization, all members are knowledgeable about the inquiry process and work together to develop information literacy concepts for lifelong learning.

Build your instructional team carefully and thoughtfully, with full knowledge of the curriculum standards to be met and the abilities of your students. Ideally, the third member of the team will contribute that ingredient that makes the collaboration really meaningful. For example, some students may benefit substantially by having a reading specialist join the team to assist them in reading and comprehending texts. Other inquiry units may be enhanced by incorporating a second subject area of the curriculum for interdisciplinary content. At other times an art, music, or drama teacher may be brought into the team to develop the product of the inquiry or important content knowledge. A technology specialist may join the team to work on computer and multimedia aspects of the inquiry. Flexibility of the team is important for providing what is needed for the best learning for the students in a particular context. Teams may need to add additional specialists at times when their expertise is needed, including experts outside the school at the public library, museums, and in the community. Teams may piggyback each other, carrying a theme developed in one subject area into another area of the curriculum or to meet another curriculum standard in the same area. For example, an investigation into science may require mathematics proofs or include a cost and risk and benefit analysis, where students are asked to design and implement a solution and evaluate the solution to a science problem. In these instances the content areas of mathematics and science substantially complement one another. Teams including both disciplines can help students through all the facets of the inquiry.

School Librarians in Information Age Schools

School librarians are the information specialists of information age schools. They provide resources that are indispensable for learning how to learn in the information age. They provide the laboratory for developing information literacy. They play a vital role on instructional teams for planning and guiding inquiry.

Although a number of schools had libraries in the early part of the 20th century, the school library only began to take an active role in student learning in the 1960s and 1970s. The term *media center* was adopted in recognition of expanding resources in the later decades of the century. The title of "librarian" was changed to "library media specialist" to acknowledge the multimedia resources that the media center provided. In some places the title "teacher librarian" is used to stress the active teaching role of the school librarian. A new title could again be conceived to recognize the information specialist role, but "school librarian" seems to capture the essence of the role in the information age school. In this book "school librarian" or simply "librarian" is used.

The school librarian is an essential member of every Guided Inquiry team. Librarians provide access to the variety of resources required for learning through inquiry. As resource experts, they provide an organized collection of materials inside the school and coordinate resources outside the school, including online materials and those available in the surrounding community in public libraries and museums, as well as subject experts. This rich information environment is established by librarians and is their unique contribution to student learning in the school.

Unfortunately the inherent role of the librarian in an information age school is often overlooked or undervalued and the library is commonly one of the first places to experience cuts when budgets are tight. Gary Hartzell (2002), a respected educator of administrators, identifies the problem as "occupational invisibility." He explains the invisibility factor thus:

[I]t [is] difficult for others both inside and outside education, to see the depth, breadth, and importance of what media specialists contribute, or should be contributing, to schools and schooling. Ironically, the nature of school library media work tends to help sustain the perception. First because librarians are engaged in empowering others, their contributions ultimately are absorbed into a teacher's lesson or a student's project . . . . Library media specialists deliver services that empower others to be successful in their jobs and their contributions get swallowed up in the activities of these people. Teachers and students take what media specialists give them and fold it into their own thinking patterns, work products, and performances. The integration is so complete that it is difficult to distinguish the extent of the specialist's contribution in the finished work. Ultimately the student sees the research project, examination success, or performance quality as something he or she puts together as an individual. Teachers empowered by library media materials and assistance ultimately see as their own the teaching act in which they employed the specialist's contributions. (p. 95)

The major school reform initiatives have neglected to envision the full potential of the school library as a vital component of information age schools. It is illogical to imagine an information age school without a fully functioning library serving as the information center. Guided Inquiry calls for rethinking the function of the school library and the librarian role in transforming K–12 education to meet the demands of the 21st century.

Implementing a Team Approach to Guided Inquiry: What Research Tells Us

We turn once again to research to inform our practice. This section discusses important findings of studies that investigated the implementation of the information search process in school settings. The studies identified elements in the school environment that contributed to problems and successes in implementation that have significant implications for implementing Guided Inquiry. The findings reveal the importance of collaboration among an instructional team and identify critical roles for each member. For a full report of these studies, see Kuhlthau (2004, ch. 9).

Participants in these studies were school librarians and teachers who attended Information Search Process Training Institutes held at Rutgers University, as well as at other locations across the United States, Canada, and Sweden. Although the length of the workshops ranged from one day to one week, each consisted of three essential components: firsthand experience in researching a topic, reflection on the process being experienced, and discussion with colleagues about ways to guide students in the process. At the close of the institutes participants showed considerable change in their perceptions of the mission of the library, understanding of the information search process, and commitment to adopting a process approach with their students. With this new perspective the librarians and teachers returned to their respective schools to implement inquiry programs based on the ISP approach, also referred to as the process approach.

In a follow-up study (Kuhlthau, 1993a) participants were sent questionnaires about the progress of their implementation of the process. Librarians and teachers were asked to respond to the following questions: What worked well? What problems did you have? What advice do you have for people starting the approach? What are your future plans for the approach in your school? After two years of collecting responses, certain patterns began to emerge.

Factors That Inhibit Success

Some programs seemed to be stalled, while others had achieved considerable success. Participants in the stalled programs cited three primary inhibitors: lack of time, confusion about roles, and poorly designed assignments (see Figure 4.1).

Implementation Inhibitors

- Lack of time
- Confusion about roles
- Poorly designed assignments

Figure 4.1. Implementation Inhibitors.

Lack of Time

Lack of time was evidenced in two forms. One was lack of student time on the task. There was not enough time for students to work through the process under the guidance of the instructional team. Second was insufficient planning time for development of team guidance and instruction. Teachers and librarians had no time set aside for planning and little time to develop the joint aspects of their teaming efforts. Essentially they assumed traditional roles because they lacked the appropriate time to be more inventive and explore ways that they might work together to help students develop skills for seeking and using information within a subject area.

Confusion of Roles

The lack of time for planning may have contributed to another problem, a basic confusion over roles. No clear notion of who was responsible for what was developed beyond the traditional roles of librarian as resource gatherer and teacher as assignment giver. There simply was not sufficient time to identify new roles. There was also no recognized or articulated role for administrators to play. In fact, most administrators were not involved in any way.

Poorly Designed Assignments

The third problem that became evident in the stalled programs was assignments that did not encourage inquiry learning. In fact, some assignments actually seemed to impede learning. Assignments were primarily designed by the teacher, with the librarian joining in sometime after initiation and frequently much later in the process. Many assignments were "added on" rather than being an essential component of the course of study and directly integrated into the subject curriculum. To make matters worse, the assignments were sometimes given at the most inconvenient time in the school year, such as the week before winter break. Even the most enlightened teachers seemed to regard library assignments as enrichment activities rather than as learning essential concepts and developing the basic skills of information literacy needed to address emerging questions.

Factors That Enable Success

It was more difficult to identify the underlying characteristics of programs that were judged to be successful. To investigate and identify the more subtle elements of successful implementation, a longitudinal case study of one program was conducted over a period of four years. Three site visits and five phone interviews took place during the study. Focus interviews during the site visits were the primary method for investigating the administrators', teachers', and librarian's perceptions of what was taking place. In the focus interviews each participant was asked to respond to the following prompts. (For further detailed description of this study see Kuhlthau, 2004, ch. 9.)

Describe your program and how it is different from what you have done before.

- What worked well?

- What problems have you encountered?

- What role did you play in the program?

- Tell an anecdote of process learning that you observed.

- What are your plans for the future of this program?

The study revealed four basic enablers of successful implementation (see Figure 4.2). They are discussed in detail below.

Implementation Enablers

- Constructivist view of learning
- Team approach to teaching
- Competence in designing process assignments
- Commitment to developing information literacy

Figure 4.2. Implementation Enablers.

Constructivist View of Learning

A mutually held constructivist view of learning compatible with the process approach that provided the foundation for actively engaging students in inquiry was an important element of success. Constructivist learning was clearly articulated and readily understood by each member of the instructional team. They agreed that students come to a learning situation not as "empty vessels" or "blank slates" but with a range of personal constructs formed from prior experience, and that learning takes place by building on what they already know. The team had a mutually accepted philosophical base from which to work.

Team Approach to Teaching

A team approach to teaching, with administrators, teachers, and school librarians playing essential roles on the instructional team, was identified as an important element of success. First and foremost, implementation was revealed as a team effort. The faculty of the school was found to have extensive experience in team instruction. The administrators fully endorsed the instructional team approach. Each member of the team had a clearly defined role to play. Genuine mutual respect and appreciation for each other as contributing members of the team was evident.

Competence in Designing Assignments

Competence in designing process assignments and in guiding student learning through those assignments was found to be another element of success. The instructional team was committed to improving learning. They were ready to experiment with methods rather than expecting to be handed a packaged formula to follow. They used their competence and expertise to design, assess, and redesign the program. They were open to innovation and ready to assume professional responsibility for designing interventions and instruction to improve student learning. They were willing to let go of old ways of doing things to take the risk of trying something new and to accept the extra work involved.

Commitment to Developing Information Literacy

A shared commitment to developing information literacy and motivating students to take responsibility for their own learning was identified as another element of success. The team was not preoccupied with "teaching for the test." They had a clear understanding that they were preparing students for higher level thinking and problem solving. They were committed to developing skills for locating and using information for lifelong learning as well as to teaching subject content.

Roles of Team Members in the Case Study School

The subject area coordinator articulated the goals and set the philosophical framework for the process approach. He explained to the instructional team how the approach fit into the curriculum and was tied to the school's goals and objectives. One school goal was to develop higher level thinking, and the coordinator explained that "the information search process is our way to achieve this goal." The coordinator articulated the constructivist view of learning and was able to describe how the ISP approach was compatible with this view, and that it was an extension and enhancement of the writing process that had been in place for a number of years.

The principal showed considerable interest in the project. He valued the ISP approach as integrating the library program across the curriculum because of the impact he observed on student learning. He was particularly impressed by the collaborative work of students. He observed that "everyone was on task" and that students were "giving each other advice." The principal saw merit in the ISP approach and advocated its adoption.

The assistant principal of the school, who was responsible for scheduling, provided the environment for teaming and the opportunity for team planning. As he stated, he "helped with the logistics." By arranging the schedule to allow for the teachers and librarian to have preparation periods at the same time, he provided the time for planning and working together during the school day.

The principal gave the project credence. He conducted required formal observations of teachers and librarians as they worked with students on projects in the school library. He showed the students the importance of the project by talking to them about their work as he met them in the course of the school day. In something of an understatement, he said his role was to "show a little bit of interest." The administrators provided the climate for teaming and the time for planning, and promoted, recognized, and rewarded faculty involved in the ISP approach.

The teachers provided the context and content. They worked in conjunction with the librarian to design the assignment to foster inquiry through the stages of the ISP. They were particularly pleased with student engagement and achievement. One veteran teacher related that, "this was one of the best experiences in my 18 years of teaching." Teachers concentrated on identifying problems, designing instructional strategies to aid students, and assessing learning.

The reading and study skills specialist guided students in using information, which was found to take more time and energy than anticipated. She served as an additional professional for coaching students in reading, note taking, and writing about emerging ideas. She was dedicated to the team approach and enthusiastically described the outcome of cooperation among the instructional team. "Everyone was doing the part he or she can do best. No one of us could do this alone." Her expertise in helping students develop the skills needed to understand information once it had been located was an important contribution to the instructional team.

Last, but certainly not least, the librarian provided the resources, defined the ISP, and was the unifying force in directing the program. The principal described her as, "the person who gets it going and keeps it on track." She initially explained the ISP to administrators, coordinators, and teachers and then spent a full year laying the groundwork for implementation. In addition, she provided a creative climate in the library. As one of the teachers said, "She wants the library used and loves it when the place is crowded." The librarian initiated and facilitated the ISP approach, keeping student learning as the focus.

In this research the identification of inhibitors and enablers provided insight into the problems and successes of implementing Guided Inquiry. A constructivist view of learning and a team teaching approach were found to underlie successful implementation. The instructional team collaborated on designing assignments that involved students in the inquiry process and developed information literacy.

Roles of the Guided Inquiry Team

Each member of the Guided Inquiry team has a role; taken together they provide a powerful learning environment for students. The effect of this mutual effort is described by a teacher who commented that, "Everyone was doing the part he or she can do best. No one of us could do this alone." The roles of administrators, librarians, and teachers inside the school and community experts outside the school combine to provide a dynamic environment for student inquiry.

Working as an instructional team is not easy. Professional training and experience enable a team to work together smoothly and to benefit from each others' expertise and talents. However, there are bound to be differences of opinion from time to time; these can actually serve to make the collaboration stronger by requiring the whole team to rethink what they are doing. This rethinking is necessary in guiding students through an extensive inquiry unit. Different people approach decision making in different ways. These many ways of looking at something make the collaboration stronger if each member of the team respects the contribution of the others on the team. Myers Briggs character and temperament types (Keirsey and Bates, 1978) may be helpful in enabling the team to become aware of different work styles that can provide balance on the work team but cause conflict if not understood. For example, some people strive for closure and may press to make decisions quickly, while others like to keep things open and may avoid making a definite decision. These two types of decision makers can be in constant conflict on a team. However, when they are aware that their differences can bring balance to the team, they can work together to move the project forward. Respect for each others' expertise and consideration of different work styles enable members of a team to build on their strengths.

The various contributors to Guided Inquiry teams play different roles, providing a rich learning environment for students. Following is a discussion of some of the roles that make Guided Inquiry a success.

Role of School Administrators

Although school administrators are not actually working members of the Guided Inquiry instructional team, they are essential to its success. Their influence is critical in all four of the enablers for successful implementation. Guided Inquiry depends on administrators who view learning as a constructive process, encourage and reward a team approach to teaching, support the staff in efforts to gain competence in designing process assignments, and are committed to fostering and developing information literacy.

The philosophy of learning of district superintendents, school principals, subject area supervisors, and curriculum coordinators establishes the learning environment and instructional climate of the school. Administrators with a constructivist view of learning are likely to support inquiry learning and promote a team approach to teaching. The school principal provides the climate for teaming and time for planning. Time for team planning and working together during the school day can be provided by coordinating the scheduled preparation periods for teachers and librarians. Subject area supervisors and curriculum coordinators who recognize that inquiry learning is tied to the curriculum goals and objectives are likely to promote an inquiry approach as an excellent way to meet curriculum standards.

School librarians take on a central role when administrators recognize the essential contribution libraries make to student learning. The contributions of the library are often folded into student and teacher success, but that should not cloud administrators' perception of their value (Hartzell, 2002). Where administrators recognize information literacy as an important life skill for their students, the milieu is right for Guided Inquiry. Administrators who realize that the ability to locate, evaluate, and use information from a variety of sources is a necessary life skill for students understand that the library is essential in the information age school.

Administrators also provide support in practical ways. They offer teachers and librarians opportunities for professional development to design and implement Guided Inquiry. Administrators give inquiry learning credence by showing interest in students' work and through informal visits as well as scheduled formal observations.

As leaders of the schools, administrators are charged with transforming schools for 21st-century learning. They provide the vision, inspiration, and rewards that sustain inquiry as an approach to learning that can revitalize their school. Too many past initiatives in collaboration have been from the bottom up, with the librarian teaming with one teacher on a curriculum unit without any direct support from or even notice by the administrator. Guided Inquiry requires top-down leadership as well as bottom-up commitment. All school personnel need to be committed for the program to be successful and sustained over time.

Role of Teachers

Guided Inquiry is successful when teachers see its value for their students. A commitment to the four enablers for successful implementation is a primary component of inquiry learning: Teachers, with a constructivist view of learning, team approach to teaching, competence in designing process assignments, and commitment to developing information literacy, are ready to collaborate with school librarians to establish Guided Inquiry.

The Guided Inquiry instructional team is made up of a school librarian and teachers. On the instructional team at least one of the teachers is a subject specialist, who defines the content and curricular objectives to meet local and national standards. This role is essential for every Guided Inquiry unit. The teacher, in consultation with the school librarian, identifies standards that may be best met by inquiry learning. One of the teacher's main responsibilities is to select the curriculum standards that the students will address and master over the course of the unit. In addition, the teachers partner with the school librarian to plan and provide intervention on content and concepts in the inquiry process. Linking the content to the curriculum standards occurs in every stage of inquiry as new issues, ideas, and questions arise.

When an interdisciplinary approach to inquiry is adopted, a second subject teacher will join the team. In secondary school, combining two subjects can offer a broad perspective on the issues and topics under investigation. It is important that all three members of the team be involved from the beginning in discussing the selection of the curriculum standards to be met and all the planning that follows. An interdisciplinary approach is natural in elementary school, where classroom teachers are responsible for many subject areas. Two classroom teachers at the same grade level may choose to collaborate on one unit of study. A problem with such collaboration in the past was the lack of materials for students in two classes to use. However, with the expanded access to resources through technology it may be more feasible to collaborate across a grade level. Two different grade level teachers may also join together, with the students studying the same topic but offering very different perspectives and approaches to the topic. In a multiage collaboration, older students can assist younger students as reading buddies or study buddies. Both groups can benefit from the information and understanding they gather throughout the process. These kinds of projects highlight the benefits of seeing not only the classroom but the school as a learning community.

Special area teachers are a great asset to the team, bringing their expertise to the inquiry of students. Music, art, and drama teachers add a creative dimension to the inquiry. Technology teachers can provide needed guidance in the use of computers, video, and film for both researching resources and producing a product. Other specialists may be available to add content expertise, such as teachers of health, careers, sports, or industrial and domestic arts. All of these teachers bring their specialization to enhancing inquiry, making it more interesting and engaging for students.

Other specialists in the school may be available to assist with reading, writing, and learning. Tailor the team to the students' needs. The third member of the team can strengthen the learning environment for specific students. Reading teachers and learning abilities specialists may be needed. They can identify problems and design differentiated instructional strategies to aid individual or groups of students.

Course assignments drive the educational program of the school. Assignments that center on inquiry go beyond fact finding to develop the higher level thinking of analysis and synthesis. Competence in designing assignments is one of the four essential enablers of successful implementation. As the initial invitation to inquiry, the assignment determines the way students proceed through the inquiry process. Designing inquiry assignments and developing intervention to guide student learning is a team effort. While each member of the instructional team has a particular specialization, all members are knowledgeable about the inquiry process and work together to develop information literacy concepts for lifelong learning.

Role of the School Librarian

The school library is the information resource center for implementing Guided Inquiry, with the school librarian as the indispensable member of the instructional team. Although the teams are flexible, with different teachers taking part in different inquiry units, the school librarian is a necessary member of every Guided Inquiry team.

Roles of the School Librarian	
Resource specialist	▪ Develops school library resources ▪ Provides Internet resources ▪ Provides contacts with community resources
Information literacy teacher	▪ Teaches concepts for information access, evaluation, and use ▪ Maintains long-term relationships with students from year to year ▪ Fosters constructivist learning environment
Collaboration gatekeeper	▪ Coordinates Guided Inquiry team ▪ Keeps communication open ▪ Uses flexible managerial skills ▪ Communicates with community

Figure 4.3. Roles of the School Librarian.

The school librarian has three main roles in Guided Inquiry: resource specialist, information literacy teacher; and collaboration gatekeeper (see Figure 4.3). As the resource specialist the school librarian provides access to resources for the inquiry both inside and outside the school. The school library provides a collection of high-quality, engaging materials that support and enhance all areas of the school, well organized for efficient access by students and teachers. The librarian, aware of changes in the curriculum, is continually updating and improving the collection to meet the needs of the students in the school as well as selecting resources available through the network of computer technology. The librarian provides access to a wide variety of well-selected multimedia resources for viewing and listening, available on-site and through the Internet. The librarian provides the contacts with local community experts in the public library, museums, and other community agencies who can share their knowledge with students.

School librarians are active participants in the implementation of the educational plan of the school. As members of the instructional team, they are involved in all phases of designing instruction, from setting goals and objectives, to designing interventions and activities, to establishing means for assessing learning. They incorporate constructivist learning theory into teaching methodology to foster individual construction and learning. As teachers of information literacy, school librarians select the standards and information literacy concepts that students will address and master over the course of each unit. Emphasis is placed on the process of learning from a variety of sources of information.

The librarian helps students understand basic information literacy concepts and develop the ability to apply those concepts in the process of information seeking. The librarian provides opportunities for students to understand the inquiry process from the inside. Students are encouraged to reflect on their own efforts and learn ways that their process might be effective in future information use. The librarian teaches students strategies for working through the stages of the inquiry process, incorporated with strategies for locating, evaluating, and using sources of information.

The school librarian acts as the "gatekeeper" of the instructional team, taking responsibility for ongoing communication with all partners to keep collaboration going throughout the inquiry process. In the case study the librarian was described as the "catalyst" for "getting it going and keeping it on track." The gatekeeper role is essential in Guided Inquiry. The librarian brings together resources from the school and from the community outside the school. The librarian's communication with experts outside the school provides extensive resources for the inquiry unit. The gatekeeper role requires considerable flexibility and managerial skill, both critical to the success of the inquiry unit.

Role of Experts in the Community

Experts in the community outside the school may be called upon to expand and enhance inquiry learning. Public librarians are natural partners, and the public library frequently is called upon to help students with their research. Unfortunately this often occurs without advance notice from the school, resulting in an overload in the public library and thus causing misunderstandings and even friction. Guided Inquiry requires that public librarians be included in the planning of inquiry units as adjunct members of the instructional team. Public librarians specializing in child and youth services may be invited to provide resources for reading, listening, and viewing to supplement the school library collection. The school librarian as gatekeeper makes these contacts in consultation with the other members of the instructional team.

In this book we emphasize the special contribution of museums to Guided Inquiry. Chapter 5 describes how these resources may be used to enhance the curriculum. Although often overlooked, museum resources can bring life and excitement to an inquiry unit. Museum staff, particularly museum educators, are valuable contributors to inquiry learning. In smaller museums where a museum educator is not on staff, the administrator or curator may be the contact person. Museums provide real objects as primary sources for students to see and sometimes even touch. In addition, online museum collections bring a world of resources to the student in the school library or classroom. These resources are highly effective for capturing students' attention and imagination at various points in the inquiry process, called zones of intervention. Field trips, actual or virtual, allow students to see specific objects or a particular collection that brings life to the inquiry at the right time in the process. A caveat is that a typical museum field trip may take on too much in one visit. Although it is tempting to try to see everything of interest, this is counterproductive. Museum visits should address a specific objective in the inquiry and serve a particular purpose. Concentrating on the part of the museum collection that specifically informs student inquiry is of significant and lasting value. These resources need to be used wisely, or they merely clutter the inquiry with extraneous material. The right resource used at the right time can bring insight and spark student learning.

It is important for public librarians and museum workers to have a clear understanding of the students' inquiry task. In addition, it is beneficial for them to understand the stages of the inquiry process and to know what stages students are in when they interact with them. The school librarian communicates this essential information to outside resources.

People who have special expertise in the subject of inquiry are another valuable outside resource. Community members who are experts may be invited to come in and share their expertise. This can be an exciting real-life experience for students. In addition, the Internet provides access to experts outside the local community, giving the students the authentic experience of communicating with someone they have read about and whose opinion they respect. Some people are willing to travel and will make a significant effort to meet with students and interact with them about their work. Outside experts can greatly enhance the authenticity of school inquiry.

Other People Who Influence Implementation of Guided Inquiry

A number of other people may influence the success and sustainability of Guided Inquiry. Parents are important stakeholders in their children's education. They are aware of the changing world and want their children to be prepared for success. Parents can be most enthusiastic supporters when they see the engagement and interest their children have in school and the learning they have achieved through Guided Inquiry. In addition, parents are a potential resource as experts who can share their life experiences.

Another influential group of stakeholders are governing officials and policy makers at local, state, and national levels. These people are involved in decisions that have a major impact on shaping schools in the 21st century. Boards of education are the primary decision makers for school policy and have great influence on how funding is allocated. It is important that alternatives to the 20th-century model be clearly understood by policy makers at all levels.

Building the Guided Inquiry Team

The information age calls for a new model, an instructional team of teachers bringing varying expertise to create a collaborative learning environment. The core Guided Inquiry team identifies members of the extended team for different tasks and portions of the inquiry process. The flexibility of the team is an important component of the new model. Who is on the Guided Inquiry team is determined by the specialization called for by the curriculum and by the specific needs of the students (see Figure 4.4). The school librarian partners with a subject teacher, and together they call on the special expertise of other staff members to provide a rich learning experience for students. The team works together during the planning and implementation of the inquiry unit. The school should be organized around a flexible team model rather than a fixed, lock-step structure for delivering all instruction. Guided Inquiry teams are built on the requirements of the curriculum and the needs of the students to provide a dynamic inquiry environment for learning from a variety of sources.

The Guided Inquiry Team

- ✓ Understands the constructivist approach
- ✓ Embraces the team approach to teaching
- ✓ Includes administrators
- ✓ Considers inquiry central to curricular learning
- ✓ Commits to developing information literacy
- ✓ Allocates time for team planning
- ✓ Defines clear roles for each team member
- ✓ Designs assignments that enable and enhance inquiry learning
- ✓ Allocates time for extended learning
- ✓ Commits to guiding students through learning
- ✓ Adopts a flexible approach
- ✓ Endorses innovation and creativity

Figure 4.4. The Guided Inquiry Team.

Throughout this book *instructional team* is used synonymously with *Guided Inquiry team*. However, the term "instructional" may be somewhat limiting. Instruction is only one of the interventions provided by the Guided Inquiry team. Chapter 9 discusses interventions carefully planned by the team to develop research competency and subject knowledge as well as fostering cooperative learning, reading comprehension, language development, and social skills.

Resources for a Rich Learning Environment

High-quality resources are a stimulus for inquiry learning. Guided Inquiry takes students beyond the predigested format of the textbook into learning from a variety of sources to construct their own understandings. Students learn to think about subject content apart from prescribed responses or preset solutions. They are guided through a process of construction that enables them to build on what they already know and to arrive at a deeper understanding of the concepts and problems underlying a subject. At the same time, they learn *how* to learn in an abundant information environment, one that is comparable to the world outside the school.

The rich learning environment begins with a collection of high-quality resources inside the school. This collection is enhanced by a wide range of resources outside the school. Guided Inquiry brings inside resources and outside resources together. Resources in the school library are expanded by materials in the community from the public library, local museums, other selected services, various sites, and experts. Resources outside the school are further expanded by connection to the World Wide Web.

There are many reasons to employ a range of resources for learning. Different types of resources provide different kinds of information. Different kinds of information lead to a more thorough investigation into a topic. For example, when students encounter sources that provide different points of view, they begin to think of information as something that may be adapted and used in a more personal way.

Different types of resources also provide different experiences for learning. When students encounter a combination of media, they begin to see how various resources reinforce each other to build their depth of understanding. Using a variety of resources opens opportunities for many ways of knowing and learning about a curriculum topic. For example, a fictional story about a historical event, an encyclopedia article with facts about the event, a video film of the event, a nonfiction account of the event, a museum exhibit of artifacts and objects from the event, and an expert's experience related to the event give students many ways of learning and building lasting knowledge about that one event.

A combination of resources provides experiences that enrich the learning environment. School libraries have incorporated audio and visual materials with books from the earliest days of the 20th century. By the middle of that century, many school libraries were granted federal funding to develop multimedia collections that transformed school libraries into media centers. The important emphasis on providing resources that offer a wide range of experiences for learning continues into 21st-century schools. Computers have extended the availability of resources enormously. They provide access to a vast collection of multimedia information from around the world.

Different Ways of Knowing

Howard Gardner's (1983) "multiple intelligences" explain that each person has some combination of eight different kinds of ability: linguistic, musical, logical-mathematical, spatial, bodily-kinesthetic, interpersonal, intrapersonal, and naturalistic. While schools have traditionally favored the linguistic and logical over the others, Gardener's work offers more comprehensive ways of thinking about human talent and potential. A wide variety of resources offer opportunities for students to employ their multiple intelligences to experiencing different ways of knowing and learning. Although many resources call for the linguistic intelligence of reading texts, others draw upon musical, kinesthetic, and naturalistic intelligences. Audio, visual, and tactile resources are incorporated with texts to make use of all the senses for a deep learning experience.

Students may have a propensity to learn from specific types of sources and strategies. Some students learn easily from books and printed materials, while others need more visual stimulation and physical activity. Concrete experiences offer opportunities for students to integrate new ideas more easily. Using a variety of resources allows students to have a chance to excel in accordance with their own innate talents. They also have opportunities to stretch their abilities and develop new ways of learning. All students benefit from using a variety of media that expand their ways of knowing. They gain experience in gleaning information from all sorts of sources. Guided Inquiry also calls upon interpersonal intelligence for engaging in the community of learners and intrapersonal intelligence for self-awareness in the inquiry process.

A good selection of materials in the school library is an important base for inquiry. However, resources outside school are just as important as those inside the school. Just as the inside sources are carefully selected, those outside the school need to be thoughtfully chosen as well.

A wealth of community resources have been underused in schools. The collection at the public library expands the school library collection of materials and increases access to computers. People in the community offer expertise that makes student inquiry come alive. Museums provide objects and artifacts that make the inquiry more real. This book particularly emphasizes museum collections as an integral resource that has been underused for inquiry learning. Museum objects and exhibits are important and easily accessible sources for inquiry learning at any grade level that are frequently overlooked.

With the abundance of information today there are ever-increasing resources available to information seekers. Guided Inquiry draws on a range of resources, from the library, to the Internet, to the community. It incorporates selected high-quality books and carefully chosen online databases with museum collections and other community resources as basic sources of information for learning. These resources may be adapted to local situations and student needs by the instructional team.

The School Library as an Inquiry Lab

The school library is an inquiry laboratory that functions as an exploring space, practice room, and workshop. It is more than a storage room for old books. The library needs to function as an active inquiry space where students and the instructional team can work together for extended periods of time. There should be areas for small groups to work together as well as a gathering place for the class as a whole. The library also needs to function as an individual learning space where individual students feel welcome to pursue their interests, questions, and independent learning.

Some people think of a library as a place for books; even architects use this notion when designing school libraries. Certainly, providing a place for a collection of books and other materials is an important part of the library function. It is important to have ample shelving and storage cabinets to hold the organized collection of materials. Materials should be easily accessible to all students. Books should be stored at a height and in an arrangement that are appropriate for the age of the students in the school. Computers should be available for individual and small group use.

But thinking of the library as an inquiry lab is a better way to plan for a facility that can accommodate and stimulate student learning. School libraries should be flexible spaces with movable chairs and tables to be arranged for all kinds of learning activities. There should be spaces for reading and study, but also need spaces for conversing. The library needs some quiet spaces for individual work and one-on-one conferencing, some spaces for conversation in inquiry circles, and some large gathering space for class instruction.

School Library Resources

The school library collection is the foundational resource for inquiry learning. The collection is made up of books; general encyclopedias and other reference materials, including special encyclopedias, dictionaries, and atlases; as well as a selection of magazines, videos, computer software, and other multimedia materials and licensed databases. Each item is carefully selected by the librarian in consultation with the teachers and students based on reviews and previews to ensure the highest quality and age appropriateness. The collection is based on the curriculum being taught in the school and is selected with inquiry units in mind. It can be thought of as a living organism that grows and changes. The areas of the collection that are highly used should be constantly replenished with new, interesting items, and old, worn materials should be replaced. The collection should be kept in good order, with catalogs for locating materials kept up to date. All of this is accomplished through the librarians' expertise, time, and attention with the aid of well-trained technical and clerical assistants.

In the 1990s some school systems were under the misconception that the Internet would replace the library and make library materials and the ability to locate and use them obsolete. Actually, the opposite has proven to be the case. Books, both fiction and nonfiction, continue to be major sources of information and ideas that students can find, evaluate, and use. Library skills, more broadly conceived as information skills or information literacy, are essential for learning in the information age. In the rush to bring technology into the schools, funds earmarked for books sometimes were diverted to the purchase and installation of computers. This unfortunate choice depleted library collections and even in some instances diminished the number of teaching and library faculty. We now see computers as a tool for information searching but not as a replacement for books or libraries. However, computers have opened the school to the outside world and provided opportunities for access to an abundance of resources.

Resources in the School Library

- Books: fiction and nonfiction
- Encyclopedias and other reference materials
- Magazines and online subscriptions
- Licensed databases
- Multimedia: videos, computer simulations

Figure 5.1. Resources in the School Library.

Guided Inquiry draws on many types of materials from the school library collection. Fiction is an important source of ideas and vicarious experience. Introducing students to engaging fiction is an effective way to offer experiences that they could not otherwise have. Literature has served this purpose throughout the ages. Through Guided Inquiry, students learn to follow up on the ideas and questions that arise from their reading of fiction, which leads them into nonfiction books and a whole range of other sources. There is a relationship between fiction and nonfiction that is important for students to become aware of and experience in their reading.

Books are essential for inquiry learning. The school library collection provides a rich assortment of reading and reference materials, including fiction, poetry, biography, information books, encyclopedias, dictionaries, atlases, and other reference books. Some of these materials are in hard copy on the library shelves and some are available online. The librarian, in consultation with teachers and administrators, will decide what to have available in house and what to access online. It is wise to have at least one general encyclopedia available in hard copy, with a number of others online. Taking advantage of statewide licensing is an efficient way to provide access to high-quality, current materials. Magazines and journals and other periodicals are available through statewide licensing arrangements with companies such as EBSCO. The librarian will need to decide which periodicals to make available in hard copy. Databases containing difficult-to-find materials that are not in books or common magazines are also available through statewide licenses. Licensed databases are an excellent resource for school libraries because they have been selected by professional librarians. These databases provide materials that are superior to and more efficient for students to use than random searches of the Internet.

Computers in schools have brought a world of resources into the school library. But we must not ignore the extensive investment in time and funding that computers require. The problems inherent in using computers in schools must be faced squarely at the start. There is an ongoing expense and effort in updating of computer hardware and keeping it running. Although computers can provide a wide range of resources outside school, the ongoing maintenance must be acknowledged and addressed. The Internet provides an abundance of information of widely varying value and accuracy. When sources are carefully selected and targeted for specific inquiry tasks, they add considerable value to the resource base. Caution must be taken not to rely too heavily on computers in Guided Inquiry. Use of computers should be kept in perspective in relation to the many other resources that are important for student learning.

Traditionally, students are guided to use encyclopedias, then books and magazines. First, encyclopedias provide an overview of a topic with basic facts and background information.

Next, informational books offer detailed facts, different perspectives, and development of ideas. Magazines provide information on current topics and issues. This sequence introduces students to the layers of information that build knowledge. Computer resources fit into this sequence. Without guidance, students often fail to see the difference between sources. They use the computer indiscriminately for all purposes, often with unsatisfactory results. With guidance, students are led to use online encyclopedias, selected periodicals, and databases through a licensed service rather than doing indiscriminate searches of random Web sites. Web sites and Web logs may be okay for students to check after they have built some knowledge about their topic from selected resources within the library collection and beyond. McNally's (2005) study of use of the Internet for inquiry projects revealed that the Internet was not as useful as students had first thought and that they used it as one source among others, inside and outside the school library. A balance of sources, incorporating online computer sources with informational texts, literature, objects, and experts, provides a rich, full experience for inquiry learning.

In Guided Inquiry we often begin with a compelling fiction story that raises many questions and leads to lots of "tell me more" topics. Sometimes a provocative film or a trip to a site or museum exhibit or an expert's story can be used as a starting point. It is essential that the starter inspire and motivate students to want to find out more. *Bud, Not Buddy* (Curtis, 1999), a favorite novel among upper elementary students, is a good example of an inquiry starter. Curtis's engaging characters entice readers to consider the time period and setting of the text, the Great Depression. An orphan boy successfully seeks to find his family, who turn out to be major players in the big band circuit of Detroit. For Guided Inquiry the text can be read aloud while engaging students in conversations about the time period. Students may raise questions about the music of the times, steam locomotives, and life during this era. They may want to know more about Brer Rabbit and orphanages, or who Herbert Hoover was, and why were there places called "Hoovervilles." When a piece of literature is rich, like Curtis's *Bud, Not Buddy,* and students are encouraged to voice their wonderings throughout the reading, their questions lead naturally into inquiry. As Bud himself states, "It's funny how ideas are, in a lot of ways they're just like seeds. Both of them start real, real small and then . . . woop, zoop, sloop before you can say Jack Robinson they've gone and grown a lot bigger than you ever thought they could" (p. 70). Using excellent literature as a starter can have such an effect on a Guided Inquiry unit.

Another example is the historical fiction text, *Fever 1793* (Halse Anderson, 2000), used in a middle school. The conversation about the readings leads to an interesting inquiry. *Fever* is the tale of a young girl, set in Philadelphia in the 1790s during the epidemic of yellow fever. Halse Anderson intricately weaves into the text many historical facts and interesting aspects of life, medicine, and race relations of the time. Using *Fever 1793* as a starter can shape the inquiry into a study comparing the life and times of the late 1700s to today. Questions arise from the text about medicine, politics, everyday life, the handling of a major health disaster, and how groups such as African Americans came together to help each other. An added benefit of quality historical fiction is that it shows that authors must research their time period deeply before writing. In this particular text Halse Anderson explains in the afterword the details of her research into this historical event. She supplies the answers to her questions, which provides the students with a model for their own inquiry. Many questions for the students to seek answers to remain, and the stage is set for an engaging Guided Inquiry unit.

Literature can be used to enliven various stages of the inquiry process. For example, inquiry can lead students into reading literature. Secondary school librarian Carol Collins uses Guided Inquiry to interest her reluctant intercity juniors in reading *The Great Gatsby* (Fitzgerald, 1925). She teams with the English teacher to guide students as they investigate the lives of popular sports figures and music performers. This inquiry project sets the stage for making the required reading more relevant to the students' lives. Once these students begin to see similarities between the lives of current pop culture figures and the characters in the novel, they become more interested in reading and discussing this work of fiction. The teacher has been amazed at the improvement in students' participation and engagement in the required reading when inquiry is undertaken to provide background knowledge.

Resources Outside the School

Contemporary learning requires that students be able to make use of resources beyond the school as well as those inside the school library. The Internet makes a vast world of resources available. Museum and community resources provide real-world applications for school-based inquiry. Experts on a subject can share special information relevant to the inquiry. Object-based learning in the classroom provides a concrete basis for abstract understandings. When students make use of varied resources such as these, the school becomes a vibrant workplace in which learning is connected to the world outside the classroom. In this way, Guided Inquiry engages students in strategies and understandings for lifelong learning.

<table>
<tr><td colspan="2" align="center">Resources Outside the School</td></tr>
<tr><td>•</td><td>Internet</td></tr>
<tr><td>•</td><td>Public library</td></tr>
<tr><td>•</td><td>Museums</td></tr>
<tr><td>•</td><td>Community resources</td></tr>
<tr><td>•</td><td>Experts</td></tr>
<tr><td>•</td><td>Objects</td></tr>
</table>

Figure 5.2. Resources Outside the School.

Using the Internet for Guided Inquiry

The Internet has opened up a world of resources for research. Every year there are more and better resources available to the general public through Internet access. However, students must learn judicious use of such resources. Too often students are left on their own with inadequate skill to evaluate them. They often copy material directly from Internet sources, some of which are of dubious accuracy and value. In Guided Inquiry the instructional team selects high-quality resources from among databases, Web sites, and online libraries and makes them available to students. Students learn to distinguish between reliable and unreliable resources. Information literacy involves understanding the kinds of information available on the Internet, discriminating between sources, and choosing those most appropriate for the task at hand.

Oppenheimer warns that, "The World Wide Web—the uber-program of the modern age—is a useful if not invaluable research source for all of us. But we all must realize that opening the Internet's door to youngsters also requires teachers to accept additional responsibilities. This does not just involve watching out for pornographic or violent material; that's the easy part. It also concerns watching what values and beliefs students develop about what knowledge is; how it's built; how it's used; and what it demands of them, as students and as citizens" (2003, p. 395). This is the difficult task that Guided Inquiry takes on.

Public Libraries

Public libraries are learning institutions. The close relationship between the public library and the school library is founded in their parallel missions. The public library serves the whole community, while the school library serves a special segment of that community. The school library collection reflects and responds to the school curriculum. The different objectives of the two institutions have often strained relations. However, the children's and youth services of the public library serve the same constituents as the school library. Partnerships between the two institutions are important for Guided Inquiry.

Three major aspects of public library services enrich inquiry learning: the collection, the facility, and the staff. We have discussed the valuable contribution of partnerships with the public library staff and the use of the public library facility, particularly at times when the school is closed and the school library is not available for students.

In this chapter we turn our attention to the public library's role in providing a rich range of resources for student inquiry. The public library collection extends and enhances the school library collection by offering students many more sources, professionally selected and organized for access. The public library also frequently provides Internet access and other computer use that is essential for students who do not have computers at home. The public library upholds its long and honored tradition of meeting the needs of those citizens who otherwise would not have access to technology. The "digital divide" is addressed in many communities by access to computer technology in the public library.

Museums

In education, museums are often overlooked as a real resource. They are designed to be places of lifelong learning. When students do not learn to access these rich resources during their school years, it is less likely that they will turn to museums later in life as places for enrichment or learning. Guided Inquiry uses museum collections as one of the main resources for a rich learning environment.

A museum is a learning institution like a library. The American Association of Museums (AAM) provides the following definitions on its Web site (www.aam-us.org.):

American museums are infinitely diverse. The AAM *Code of Ethics for Museums* notes that their common denominator is making a "unique contribution to the public by collecting, preserving, and interpreting the things of this world." That code also acknowledges the variety of sizes and types of museums: "Their numbers include both governmental and private museums of anthropology, art history and natural history, aquariums, arboreta, art centers, botanical gardens, children's museums, historic sites, nature centers, planetariums, science and technology centers, and zoos."

The International Council of Museums (ICOM) defines a museum as:

> A non-profitmaking, permanent institution in the service of society and of its development, and open to the public, which acquires, conserves, researches, communicates and exhibits, for purposes of study, education and enjoyment, material evidence of people and their environment.

The federal government, in the Museum and Library Services Act, defined a museum as:

> A public or private nonprofit agency or institution organized on a permanent basis for essentially educational or aesthetic purposes, which, utilizing a professional staff, owns or utilizes tangible objects, cares for them, and exhibits them to the public on a regular basis.

These definitions make clear that museums are educational institutions. They exist to collect, preserve, and share information about objects with scholars and the general public. Museums hold objects in trust for the public and have the mission to share the research they conduct with the public. It is unfortunate when students are deprived of museums as learning resources and when schools neglect to use the information available in museums. In a democratic society, museums should not be treated as elitist institutions, but should be as accessible to all as are public libraries.

Museums have much in common with libraries. Both institutions exist to care for and make accessible a collection that is useful for the increase of knowledge. Through the Museum and Library Services Act, the U.S. government acknowledged this shared mission and created the Institute of Museum and Library Services (IMLS) as the primary funding agency for the nation's museums and libraries. The IMLS states its mission as "to grow and sustain a 'Nation of Learners' because life long learning is essential to a democratic society and individual success." A review of featured projects supported by IMLS (www.imls.gov/profiles/) reveals the learning potential when schools, libraries, and museums collaborate. People outside of the museum field may not be aware of the museum as a research institution. Each museum has a special emphasis, with a mission to provide accurate and up-to-date information about the subject of its collection. Because museums are conservative institutions, they are conscientious about the accuracy of information that they distribute about their collections.

The objects in museums may be works of art, natural or scientific objects, cultural objects, or objects of historical interest. When museum professionals speak of objects they may be referring to photographs, documents, images, and other ephemera, such as ticket stubs, menus, and playbills that document events or record information about a particular time period. The primary way of providing access to museum objects and the scholarly discussion of experts has historically been the museum exhibition. Because exhibitions are physically restricted to a local audience or those who can physically visit them, museums are developing Web resources to expand access to their collections. The Internet is increasingly providing a different type of access to museum collections and research. This access does not take the place of a visit to the museum and an encounter with actual collections, but provides information that is very valuable.

A museum may be thought of as a resource in three ways: as a collection, as exhibits, and as programs. Exhibitions have traditionally been the way that museums provide access to the objects and information contained in their collections. Increasingly, museums have begun to provide direct access to their collections online. The digital collection usually contains images of and scholarly information about the objects held at the museum. Museums often also offer public programs for various audiences. These programs have been mainly available locally to people who can visit the museum. Increasingly, programs for school, family, and adult audiences are also available on the museums' Web sites. Museums, then, can be a resource for learning locally, regionally, nationally, and even internationally.

Museums on the Internet

When considering sources for Guided Inquiry, it is essential that students have access to high-quality, accurate information. Increasingly, museums, archives, and libraries are creating Web sites at which the public can access information that was formerly only available to high-level scholars in a given field. Many of these Web sites include sections specially designed for use by students, teachers, and other educators. These Web sites are valuable assets for Guided Inquiry. For instance, when studying the Underground Railroad, students and teachers can visit the National Underground Railroad and Freedom Center's Web site at www.freedomcenter.org. This is a museum in Cincinnati, Ohio. If you live nearby you can visit the museum and take advantage of its programs for students. However, if you do not live in that area, you can find useful and accurate information on the Web site, such as a timeline, a list of Underground Railroad sites in each state, and stories of people associated with the Underground Railroad. Since the museum has a mission to study the Underground Railroad, you can be fairly certain that the information found at the museum's Web site is accurate and reflects current scholarship. The same cannot be said for many other sites on the Web.

All accredited museums have a mission statement that will give you a good idea whether a particular museum studies the subject that is relevant to a particular inquiry. It is impossible to list every museum with good Web sites for students and teachers, as museums are continually updating, revising, and improving their Web presence.

A few museums, archives, and online libraries have Web sites that have been so consistently of high quality and easy to use that they are worth listing here:

- The Library of Congress (www.loc.gov) has an extensive digital collection that includes sections designed especially for students and teachers. Most notably, American Memory (http://memory.loc.gov/ammem/index.html) provides historical photographs, sound recordings, and images of objects in the collection that are organized in easy-to-use topics such as African American History, Architecture/Landscape, Environment/Conservation, and Government/Law. The site includes lesson plans and ideas for using the collection.

- The National Archives (www.archives.gov) has a collection of historical documents, letters, photographs, and other primary sources. In addition to the Declaration of Independence and the Constitution, the collection includes famous photographs by Ansel Adams and Dorothea Lange and other important documents. You can order copies of any of these documents for educational use.

- The Smithsonian Institution (www.si.edu) is a network of museums on a variety of subjects. The main Web site can take you to the Web site of each individual museum. In addition to the well-known National Museum of American History, National Museum of Natural History, and the Air and Space Museum, the Smithsonian includes museums of African art, Asian art, American art, postal history, and more. The Smithsonian has a main Web site for education (www.smithsonianeducation.org) that includes lesson plans for using objects in the Smithsonian's collections.

• The American Association of Museums has a directory of member museums that is a useful index of museums organized by subject or geographic location (http://iweb. aaam-us.org/membership/MemberDirectorySearch.aspx). These museums are accredited by the AAM, which guarantees a high level of professionalism and accuracy.

Object-Based Learning

Object-based learning is the main method of teaching used by museum educators. Objects can also be valuable resources for learning in the school environment through Guided Inquiry. One only has to watch PBS's *Antiques Roadshow* to see the intrinsic interest that objects can hold. It is not only the monetary value of the objects that intrigues us, but also the stories that the experts can tell about them. The use of objects is key to providing experiences for engaging multiple intelligences. Using objects in teaching provides opportunities for spatial understanding, bodily-kinesthetic ways of knowing, and other intelligences, depending on the object. Using an object engages the senses, which increases interest and leads to individuals creating a personal connection to the learning. As the students engage in sensory exploration of an object related to the subject being investigated, they make their own observations and connections. Objects are concrete. When students manipulate the objects, they can use the physical information to inform and help develop abstract ideas.

Objects can create a valuable link to the world outside of the school and so they are a natural way to encourage "third space." Each object will initiate different reactions in different people, depending on peoples' experiences and association. Often students have an easier time of speaking about an object than about other information. In object based learning, observations and associations with the object are acceptable so long as they are grounded in what is observable about the object.

Many educators are familiar with using objects as props in teaching. When objects are used as props, they are not the focus of an investigation, but they may provide a tangible connection to a metaphor related to what the instructor wants to convey. Props bring interest and color to what might otherwise be a dry subject.

For instance, at the beginning of the year a teacher might use a basket as a metaphor for the community of learners. She tells the students to notice that the basket is made up of individual reeds that are woven together to create an object of use and beauty. The classroom community is like the basket, and the individuals are like the reeds. The individuals in the class will work together, helping one another at different points. Each individual is important to the whole. The reeds are woven together in a pattern. This pattern is like the rules in a class. If one reed is missing or not working according to the pattern, the whole basket is affected. When the pattern is followed and the reeds work together, the basket is complete. Just like in the classroom, when all of the individuals cooperate and work together, we can create a wonderful learning environment.

This object lesson requires students to understand a minimal amount about the actual basket in question. The basket is there to create a more vivid image for the students. Certainly the metaphor of the basket provides concrete imagery for the students to consider the more abstract idea of a community of learners and why rules are important in it. The use of a prop provides a concrete way to illustrate a point.

The same basket could be used for an object-based lesson. An object-based lesson starts with simple collection of data on the physical characteristics of the object. After the data have been gathered, the students can analyze and interpret them according to what the subject of the inquiry is. An object may be interpreted according to scientific study (materials), historical or cultural information (who made it, when and why), mathematical information (dimension, volume, density), or aesthetic or artistic consideration (design).

A social studies class studying Native American life before and during the colonial era might use an American Indian basket as an inquiry starter. The Guided Inquiry team might start by passing the basket around and asking each student to say a different word to describe the basket. These words can be listed on a white board. The students then categorize the words according to which are facts and which are personal observations. Then the students may be divided into four groups. Each group is asked to draw two columns on a paper and list facts in one column and observations in the other. After this task is completed, the students raise a question about the basket, such as, "Who made it and for what purpose?" Students try to answer the question using evidence from the fact side of the chart to support their claim. At the end of the exercise the students write what questions they still have about the basket and things they do not know. The groups consult other sources to investigate their remaining questions and prepare a presentation to report back to the whole class on what they found out.

An object may be explored in relation to scientific, historical, and design considerations. A student can explore a man-made object to determine how or why it was made, what materials or processes were used in its production, why it was first invented, or other purposes for which it could be used. Natural objects can be explored for information about the material, how it was formed, what uses it could be to people, and its relationship to other known objects.

The use of objects in inquiry helps make an abstract idea concrete. For example, mathematics classes in elementary and middle school often study tessellation patterns by reading about tessellation and drawing the patterns. Students understand tessellations much more easily by manipulating pattern blocks onto patterns from a book. What is not made clear about tessellations by using the pattern blocks is where a person might encounter tessellations in the world and why anyone might be interested in them. By manipulating actual ceramic tiles, students' senses are engaged physically and the concrete experience helps to make sense of a complex subject. An authentic object in a real-world setting holds greater interest than abstract ideas or classroom props. The pattern blocks are useful props for practicing tessellations, but they are not nearly as interesting as the real tiles or the artwork. Guided Inquiry opens up these topics for students to investigate and share with the class as a community of learners. For example, by finding photos of tiles in La Alhambra castle in Spain or another real-world setting, the students can be inspired by the wonder and beauty of the patterns. By investigating the artwork of M. C. Escher, the students can see how an artist played with tessellations. Museum visits either physically or virtually can bring real-world authenticity to abstract concepts. Objects have the power to inspire students, to demonstrate real-world settings for abstract ideas, and to provide cultural context for learning.

Community Resources

The local environment can provide many resources for bringing the outside world into the school to enrich the learning environment. This is crucial to the relevance of learning. The school should not exist in a vacuum without a connection to the community in which it is situated and the greater world beyond. By taking students outside the school to visit community resources and by bringing experts from the community into the school, students can make connections between what they are learning and life beyond the school. When students' real life is disconnected from their school life, they are not intrinsically motivated to learn the subject, and they need external motivations. Community resources such as museums, government agencies, and businesses can provide places for fieldwork to be done and from which experts can visit the school to work with students and the Guided Inquiry team.

Museums as Community Resources

It is not a new idea to plan field trips in conjunction with a unit of study. Teachers often consider scheduling a field trip to a museum, historical site, zoo, botanical garden, or nature center when planning a unit. However, the museum is often an afterthought. The museum is treated as a destination vaguely connected to the subject being taught. Often field trips are considered the prize for completing a unit of study. For this reason, field trips may be considered frivolous time out of the classroom. Administrators or overburdened teachers will often cut a field trip if additional time is needed to prepare for classroom activities or testing.

In Guided Inquiry, a field trip is integral to the inquiry process. Students may visit a museum exhibit at the beginning of a unit of study for an introduction to the variety of ideas about a certain subject. In that case the museum is a jumping off point for students to begin to formulate their questions and wonderings. A group of students may visit an exhibition to gather information just as they would from a library source. To use a museum exhibition as a resource effectively, the Guided Inquiry team must carefully plan and prepare students before making a museum visit.

Museum exhibits contain information on many different subjects. Exhibitions tell their stories through objects, images, photographs, and text written by experts knowledgeable in that field. Because exhibits are densely packed with information, it is better to visit one exhibit at a time than to attempt to visit an entire museum. Students can gain the most from visiting an exhibit when a member of the Guided Inquiry team previews the exhibit and considers a strategy for using it with them. It may be that only part of an exhibit is pertinent to the inquiry. It may be that the exhibition is so large that students should divide into small groups, each group concentrating on gathering information about one aspect of the subject. When they return to school the groups can form inquiry circles for sharing the information they have gleaned.

Often museums employ education staff who can assist the Guided Inquiry team and provide support materials for the exhibitions. Museums also often have information about their exhibitions and collections available on their Web sites. Their Web sites often also offer materials for teachers to use as background and lesson plans for pre-visit and post-visit activities. When exhibits are used in a more integrated manner, the students regard them as a learning tool and not just as a day out of the classroom.

Creating a Link with the Community

Other community resources can make excellent field visit destinations for Guided Inquiry. A class or small group could visit government offices, local businesses, or utilities. To make the most of these field trips, the Guided Inquiry team and students should meet to decide the purpose of the trip and prepare for their work. Will the students interview people that they meet? What questions will they ask? Will the students gather information by observation? How will they record the information they gather? This kind of focused field trip is part of the inquiry process. The inquiry circle jobs presented in chapter 3 may help the group focus on how to distribute the tasks needed accomplish their work.

For example, a middle school social studies class studying immigration and the procedures for gaining citizenship might visit the local government office where immigrants apply. To prepare for the visit the students consider questions about how an immigrant applies for citizenship. What is the process? What are the challenges? A visit to the office gives a more visceral understanding of what it might be like to apply for citizenship. Is the environment welcoming or confusing? What services are available for people in this situation? A clerk in this office could be interviewed about the application process. This "expert" may also have stories to tell about interacting with people going through the process. Stories have the power to engage students emotionally in a way that makes the process more real. A civics lesson then has more meaning than a list of steps in a process. Inquiry circle conversations about the experience are an excellent means of reflecting on the experience and raising questions for further inquiry.

Bringing in Experts

Experts are an underutilized resource in the school. They can be called on to give a short lecture on a subject related to an inquiry unit. Experts in the subject of the Guided Inquiry can give pertinent information at the point when it is needed. The advantage of using an expert rather than written sources is that students can interact with the person, asking questions and carrying on conversation. This kind of presentation can be engaging and informational as well as informal. Many members of the community are willing to do a short presentation on their work or a hobby related to a unit of study. Parents and friends of the school can contribute to Guided Inquiry in this way. Museums often have staff members who are willing to provide this type of outreach.

For the middle school social studies immigration unit example in the previous section, an expert who could be invited to speak to the class might be an immigrant who is currently applying for citizenship or someone who has recently gone through the process. This expert could talk not only about the steps in the process, but also about how it feels to apply for citizenship. He or she could answer questions about what challenges and opportunities were encountered and speak about his or her experiences and the emotional aspects of the process. Students who have an opportunity to interact with such an expert would benefit from an insider's experience of this citizenship lesson rather than merely memorizing the steps in the process. This experience would bring seeking citizenship to life.

Experts can also be used for more long-term projects, providing mentoring and apprentice opportunities. For instance, if working on a filmmaking, journalism, or exhibition design project, it would be beneficial to have an expert come to work with the students to provide assistance on an ongoing basis.

The Guided Inquiry team can identify possible experts during planning. They may already know of people who have expert knowledge or experiences to share. An expert may be a local artist, a person with a special collection or talent, or someone with significant experiences. The instructional team can call on friends or parents to share interests or hobbies related to the subject of inquiry. At the beginning of the inquiry unit, the team can prepare a short survey for family members to indicate interests and willingness to talk to the class. Often people may not consider their own hobbies or vocations valuable expertise unless asked specifically about them. The librarian may keep a record of experts related to curriculum content who were willing to share in this way in the past. The teacher may send home a parent survey at the beginning of the year to find out about parents' otherwise unknown expertise. The survey results could be integrated into planning for inquiry units during the year.

Using the Range of Resources for Guided Inquiry

When the full range of resources is used for Guided Inquiry, with the school library as the inquiry laboratory, a powerful learning synergy is evident. An example from a third-grade class studying scientific classification demonstrates this synergy. This inquiry unit took place over several class periods. To start the inquiry, an expert from the community was introduced to the class to share his extensive and impressive collection of shells. Students were given an opportunity to ask questions about the shells. "Where did you find them? How do you organize your collection? How did you get started collecting? What is your favorite one?" The expert talked about how he went from just picking up shells he liked to creating a collection that was organized and complete.

The next sessions were held in the school library, with students sitting in small groups or inquiry circles at tables in the center of the library. Each inquiry circle was given a group of shells and asked to come up with a list of physical characteristics that could be used to sort the shells. This task is very simple because the students could interact with the shells and list simple characteristics such as size, shape, color, texture, and design. Then the students were asked to choose one of these characteristics and sort the shells. Here it was evident that having the actual shells to sort was helpful, as they defined more specific categories such as rough, smooth, and rough-smooth. As one student said, "At first we just had rough and smooth, but then some of the shells did not fall neatly in either category. We decided to create a new category for those shells." The exercise made the students consider the categories more deeply and required critical thinking and cooperative work.

The teacher then introduced the idea of scientific classification. Scientists sort living things by their physical characteristics in much the same way the students had sorted the shells. Animals that have shells are called mollusks. Mollusks can be separated into two categories, gastropods, those that have one shell, and bivalves, those that have two shells. The teacher then asked the students to sort the shells by these categories. To help them, the librarian showed where they could find field guides to shells in the library. Each circle collected the data about the shells at their table. The data from each inquiry circle were then compiled as a bar graph.

At the end of this session students were asked to review what they had learned about shells. They were also asked what else they would like to learn. The librarian listed their questions on a white board. The questions included: "Where do these shells come from? Where can I find shells like this? Are these shells worth anything? What are the animals that live in these shells like? Do people use shells for anything?" It was determined that each inquiry circle would take one of these questions to investigate.

Students were given several more sessions in the library to investigate their questions. They used encyclopedias, atlases, and informational books. They were encouraged to share information relevant to other inquiry circles as they found it.

They decided to create a small exhibition of what they had learned about classification of mollusks and invite parents to come. The students in each inquiry circle worked together to create their exhibition. They created labels with information about their shells, placed objects on plastic cup pedestals, and cut colorful paper to create backgrounds. Parents and family members were invited to the opening of the exhibit and students acted as the expert explainers for the family visitors. The students explained what they had learned to other classes in the school, who were invited to visit the exhibition.

Guided Inquiry has the power to excite students about using resources for learning. The Guided Inquiry team selects a variety of sources for each inquiry unit that enhance the content of the curriculum and develop specific information skills and concepts. In addition, the team selects sources that match the learning level of the students while challenging them to improve and expand their literacy skills.

The school library collection provides the basis for each inquiry unit. The Guided Inquiry team first selects from a variety of media in the school library. Next the team considers sources outside the school that will enhance both students' knowledge of the subject and their understanding of the range of sources available. Using the Internet opens access to a broad range of information outside the school. The Guided Inquiry team selects relevant, high-quality databases and Web sites from the Internet.

Sources from the community enliven the inquiry process. Public libraries and museums provide accurate, reliable information from varied sources. Students learn to glean information from less common sources, such as objects, photographs, and documents. Field trips to the public library, local museums, and other community resources such as government offices or businesses can be arranged at critical points during the inquiry process. Experts on the topic can be invited from the community to share their knowledge.

The Guided Inquiry team introduces students to a range of rich learning resources and guides them through inquiry learning. The varied sources enliven the project and help to prepare students for the kind of inquiry they will encounter in the world outside school.

Information Literacy Through Guided Inquiry

When students come in as freshman they think that research is just another requirement. 'You go out on your own and you do it. Research is something you are assigned to do.' By the time they are juniors they have a sense of ownership and think of research as a life skill. As seniors they have confidence in doing it themselves. They see research as an integral skill.
—high school principal

Many school librarians have adopted information literacy as the watchword of their contribution to the education of students. However, teachers and administrators are often confused about just what information literacy is and how it is different from computer literacy or media literacy, and why it is important. What is information literacy? How do students acquire it? How important is it?

Call for a New Type of Literacy

In the late 1980s, librarians in many countries around the world began to notice that a new literacy was needed to access and use information sources in the rapidly growing technological information environment. The term *information literacy* began to be commonly applied to this type of ability. The American Library Association responded by organizing the President's Committee on Information Literacy, headed by Patricia Breivik, with representatives from all segments of education. The main purpose of the committee was "to define information literacy within the higher literacies and its importance to student performance, lifelong learning and active citizenship." The final report is a clear statement of information literacy that contains the following description of an information age school:

The school would be more interactive, because students, pursuing questions of personal interest, would be interacting with other students, with teachers, with a vast array of information resources, and the community at large to a far greater degree than they presently do today. One would expect to find every student engaged in at least one open-ended, long-term quest for an answer to a serious social, scientific, aesthetic, or political problem. Students' quests would involve not only searching print, electronic, and video data, but also interviewing people inside and outside of school. As a result, learning would be more self-initiated. There would be more reading of original sources and more extended writing. Both students and teachers would be familiar with the intellectual and emotional demands of asking productive questions, gathering data of all kinds, reducing and synthesizing information, and analyzing, interpreting, and evaluating information in all its forms.

In such an environment, teachers would be coaching and guiding students more and lecturing less. They would have long since discovered that the classroom computer with its access to the libraries and databases of the world is a better source of facts than they could ever hope to be. The would have come to see that their major importance lies in their capacity to arouse curiosity and guide it to a satisfactory conclusion, to ask the right questions at the right time, to stir debate and serious discussion, and to be models themselves of thoughtful inquiry. (American Library Association, 1989, p. 8)

At the time this description of an information age school was written it was considered a dream for the future. This picture views information literacy as embedded in an information-rich inquiry environment.

Information Literacy Standards

A decade later the American Association of School Librarians (AASL) and the Association for Educational Communications and Technology (AECT) published information literacy standards for student learning as part one of *Information Power: Building Partnerships for Learning* (AASL and AECT, 1998). This publication defines information literacy in three standards, with indicators of students who have achieved them:

Standard 1: The student who is information literate accesses information efficiently and effectively.

Indicators: recognizes the need for information; recognizes that accurate and comprehensive information is the basis for intelligent decision making; formulates questions based on information needs; identifies a variety of potential sources of information; develops and uses successful strategies for locating information;

Standard 2: The student who is information literate evaluates information critically and competently.

Indicators: determines accuracy, relevance and comprehensiveness; distinguishes among fact, point of view and opinion; identifies inaccurate and misleading information; selects information appropriate to the problem or question at hand.

Standard 3: The student who is information literate uses information accurately and creatively.

Indicators: organizes information for practical application; integrates new information into one's own knowledge; applies information in critical thinking and problem solving; produces and communicates information and ideas in appropriate formats

Two additional areas of the AASL standards are independent learning and social responsibility.

A Concepts Approach to Information Literacy

Guided Inquiry takes into account the ALA *Presidential Committee on Information Literacy Final Report* (1989) and the information literacy standards developed by AASL and AECT (1998). However, in Guided Inquiry information literacy augments these in several important ways. First, Guided Inquiry takes a concept approach to information literacy. Second, it integrates these information literacy concepts into inquiry units in the same way that curriculum standards are met through inquiry learning.

Certain basic information literacy concepts underlie the wide range of information-seeking tasks. The concepts approach presented here has been developed specifically for the Guided Inquiry program. These concepts are introduced, reinforced, developed, and applied throughout students' school years in an inquiry learning environment. The concepts defined in this chapter are transferable to other situations of information seeking and use.

All three areas of the AASL information literacy standards—information literacy, independent learning, and social responsibility—are developed through Guided Inquiry. This chapter concentrates on the three standards that emphasize access, evaluation, and use of information. Guided Inquiry introduces general concepts that underlie the ability to locate, evaluate, and use library materials and the wide range of resources available through digitized information technology and in the local community. (See Figure 6.1, p. 80) Understanding these basic concepts provides students with the foundation for independent inquiry that is necessary to information literacy. These concepts are developed gradually over the course of students' prekindergarten–12 education.

Concepts for Locating, Evaluating, and Using Information

Guided Inquiry promotes a high degree of independence in searching for, selecting, and using information over the course of the students' schooling. A conceptual approach to teaching information skills is adopted to introduce students to underlying concepts that are transferable to a wide range of situations and contexts. The program does not attempt to teach all there is to know about information searching and information technology. There are many thorough texts available that describe methods and lessons for teaching detailed information and library skills that you may choose to supplement this program to meet the specific needs of your students. The Guided Inquiry information literacy concepts are a foundation for developing high levels of proficiency and for adapting to new systems and sources that are emerging at a rapid pace. These concepts can be built over the years by integrating your school library program with the curriculum through Guided Inquiry.

Information Literacy Concepts	
LOCATE	• Library as lab for information literacy • Trails and paths—browsing, monitoring, chaining, differentiating, extracting • Types of searches—preliminary, exploratory, comprehensive, summary
EVALUATE	• Evaluating formats for reading, listening, viewing, and experiencing • Structure gives clues for evaluating sources • Five characteristics for evaluating sources—expertise, accuracy, currency, perspective, quality
USE	• Determining importance, relevance, and pertinence • Forming a focus • Deciding what is enough • Managing inquiry—taking notes, recording references • Interpreting facts and organizing ideas • Sharing with a community of learners

Figure 6.1. Information Literacy Concepts.

Concepts for Locating

The fundamental concept of access is that the vast and various sources of information may be organized to enable a person to locate a specific piece of information or particular material. The main concepts related to locating information specifically developed in Guided Inquiry are the library as lab for information literacy, trails and paths, and types of searches. (See Figure 6.2.) These concepts provide students with a basic understanding of how information is organized to enable people to locate the materials and information that they want and to access them from a library or information system.

Concepts for Locating

- Library as lab for information literacy
- Trails and paths: browsing, monitoring, chaining, differentiating, extracting
- Types of searches: preliminary, exploratory, comprehensive, summary

---

Figure 6.2. Concepts for Locating.

Library as a Lab for Information Literacy

The school library is an integral part of an information age school. It provides a wide range of resources for learning and serves as an inquiry lab. These two functions are essential components for learning in the information age. The school library provides a collection of materials that supports and enhances the curriculum and facilitates access to the vast information resources outside the school, on the Internet and in the community. A critical function of the school library, however, is as a laboratory for learning how to locate, evaluate, and use information in a wide range of situations. Guided Inquiry implements the school library as a lab for information literacy.

The school library is the ideal place for students to learn the basics of information literacy and to apply and practice their knowledge. Digital libraries and online databases are rapidly transforming access to materials previously only available in libraries. Students also learn the difference between an organized collection that has been selected and classified by librarians and information specialists and the vast information accessible on the World Wide Web. Understanding the concepts underlying organization for access is important for taking full advantage of the resources of traditional libraries, digitized online collections, and the Web.

An Organized Collection

An organized collection is based on a classification system that is commonly a combination of alphabetical and numerical codes that provide access to the materials in the collection. The school library is an excellent laboratory for learning how a classification system works. The Dewey Decimal Classification System is an example of one classification system. When students think of Dewey Classification as a model of the ways to classify information and materials so that specific items may be retrieved, they can adapt this knowledge to other systems of classification. Students can be led to think of other classification systems that they know, such as the organization of a supermarket, department store, newspaper, magazine, or sites they access to download music to their iPods. One problem with "teaching Dewey" is that unless a concept approach is used, students have difficulty transferring their knowledge to other classifications systems, such as Library of Congress, indexes in reference sources, indexes to periodicals, or the organization of an online database. Understanding the concepts of classification facilitates transference to other systems, both online digitized collections and in-house print collections.

Title and Author Access: When You Know the Name

Title and author access are important features of a classification system. This is the most straightforward means of access. The main concept is that when one knows the title of a book or other specific material, finding it in an organized collection is a fairly simple task. Titles and authors are arranged in alphabetical order. An author's fiction books will be together on a library shelf or in a digitized collection and listed together in a catalog. Books can be located by looking up the title or the author in the catalog. Alphabetizing beyond the first letter is a complex skill that enables title and author access.

Subject Access: Words That Lead to Information

The most important and commonly used concept for locating sources in an organized collection is subject access. Subject access provides the location of materials on a topic without knowing the precise title or the specific author of the source. Subject access is a key concept in inquiry. Guided Inquiry provides sequential interventions for developing students' understanding of concepts underlying subject access such as keywords, subject headings, and search terms that facilitate locating information. Students often have difficulty locating materials by subject. The term that they use may not be the term used in the library catalog or in the online database. Librarians find that students' online searches are commonly seriously flawed, consisting of natural language searches rather than Boolean connectors, which lead to more relevant information (Whelan, 2006).

Many students think that every term may be used to locate information. They often interpret not finding something as an indication that there is nothing on that topic. They need to learn to think of alternative terms that may be appropriate subject headings and search terms. Keyword searching requires the identification of descriptors. When students are guided to find out about their topic in general reference sources, such as an encyclopedia and dictionary, early in an inquiry process, they identify who, what, when, and where in relation to their topic. The answers become descriptors that can be used as subject headings when they are ready to search catalogs, periodical indexes, indexes in books, and other access tools.

A common problem identified by librarians is that periodicals, journals, encyclopedias, and informational books are often overlooked. Many students' research is reduced to Google and Internet searches. As one librarian noted, "In short, kids were going to their favorite search engines, typing poorly constructed searches and sorting through the thousands of hits they got" (Whelan, 2006).

In Guided Inquiry, as students progress through the stages of the inquiry process and learn more about their topics, they are guided to become aware of search terms, keywords, and subject headings that describe more precisely what they are looking for. Their information horizon is expanded by understanding evolving subject access through the stages of the inquiry process and by gaining greater familiarity with a wide range of quality resources.

Indexes: Tools That Lead to Information

Understanding the concept of subject access is a good foundation for learning that indexes are tools that apply subject access for locating important sources that otherwise may be difficult to find, such as periodicals and journals. Indexing is a fundamental concept that underlies locating information in a whole range of sources that are not in a library catalog, as well as for locating information within sources. In Guided Inquiry children in the third through fifth grades are introduced to the concept of indexing by using indexes in books to find specific information. When there is not an entire book devoted to a topic, many young students assume that there is no information on that topic. Even after determining the citation that pertains to the specific information needed, students may have difficulty locating the information on the page. When middle school students turn to a page in a book listed in an index, many expect to see a heading or subheading on the topic. If they do not immediately notice an indication of the topic, they often assume there is no reference to the topic on the page. Students need to understand that an index lists insignificant references to a topic as well as substantial information. Older students become more proficient at using subheadings in indexes. They learn that it takes some digging to find the useful information. Over time, through instruction and experience, students learn to use indexes for locating specific information.

Trails and Paths: Finding the Way

Guided Inquiry encourages students to think of inquiry as a journey; they need to find a trail through the information. The path that they choose may not be the same one that another student would follow. The choices they make along the way about what information is important and interesting forges their trail from source to source.

The concept of trails and paths helps students to find their way through information. Guided Inquiry introduces students to strategies developed in information science research. The concept of following a trail or path though the information helps students develop the notion of a search strategy. Students develop expertise in locating information through their understanding of the information-seeking concepts of *browsing, monitoring, chaining, differentiating,* and *extracting* (Ellis, 1989).

Browsing is semi-directed searching in an area of potential interest. In an extensive study of browsing, Rice, McCreadie, and Chang define browsing as "the process of exposing oneself to a resource space by scanning its content and structure, possibly resulting in awareness of unexpected or new content or paths in that resource" (2001, p. 258). Browsing incorporates looking through collections of materials in the library and scanning digitized collections and online sources. It is a good way to get a sense of possibilities at the beginning of the inquiry process. It is akin to a preliminary search for offering ideas of ways to shape the inquiry. In Guided Inquiry young children are made aware of their own browsing as a strategy for finding interesting things to read and facts to report. Older students apply their knowledge of the structure of sources for browsing through tables of contents and indexes and their understanding of subject access by using keywords and subject headings to scan for possible leads and ideas.

Monitoring is maintaining awareness of developments in a field through regularly following particular sources (Ellis, 1992). It involves identifying a few core sources and checking them from time to time to see if anything pertains to the area of interest. Monitoring is a particularly good strategy when the area of inquiry is a current topic and the inquiry is expected to take place over an extended period of time. In Guided Inquiry monitoring is introduced as a strategy for inquiry units that require current information and are studied over several months. Students may be alerted ahead of time to keep an eye on a certain topic to prepare for an intensive inquiry project. For example, students in fifth grade may monitor weather patterns over several months to track changes. Older students may monitor a particular news story as it unfolds.

Chaining is a well-established search strategy in library and information science that involves following up on leads from citations in sources that have been useful. References in useful materials are checked as leads to other sources that may also be of use. The references in one source provide a trail or path to other sources on the same topic. In Guided Inquiry young children make early use of chaining by looking for books by a favorite author. This sets the stage for applying chaining in middle and secondary school.

Differentiating is using differences between sources as a filter on the nature and quality of the material. It involves comparing and selecting sources by noticing differences between the quality, expertise, accuracy, currency, and perspective of the information within the sources (discussed in this chapter in the section on ways to evaluate sources). The sources students select and the choices they make through differentiating depend on their prior experience and former constructs. Guided Inquiry helps students learn how sources differ and ways to make good choices for their inquiry.

Extracting is systematically working through a particular source to identify material of interest. Bates (1989) uses the metaphor of berry picking to describe how people select information from here and there. As in berry picking, not everything is extracted from a source; only some items of information and certain ideas are selected for use. What is extracted from one source leads the path to the next source of information. In Guided Inquiry students learn that selecting information to extract from a source takes place all the way along the inquiry process and not only at the end of a search when they are preparing to present their learning.

Many online systems incorporate these strategies in their search capabilities. As Choo explains:

If we visualize the World Wide Web as a hyperlinked information system distributed over numerous networks, most of the information seeking behaviors categories in Ellis's model are already being supported by capabilities available in common web browsers. Thus a user could use the browser to reach a search engine to locate sources of interest (starting); follow hypertext links to related information resources in both backward and forward – linking directions (chaining); scan the web pages of the sources selected (browsing); bookmark useful sources for future reference and visits (differentiating); subscribe to e-mail based services that alert the user of new information or developments (monitoring) and search a particular source or site for all information on that site on a particular topic (extracting). (2006, p. 62)

Students who understand these strategies are prepared to make full use of the search capabilities of the technological information environment. Guided Inquiry prepares students to develop their own search strategy for finding their way through a vast amount of information that is fundamental to information literacy.

Four Types of Searches: Searching Along the Way

Guided Inquiry emphasizes developing thoughts and ideas about a topic, issue, or problem as the inquiry progresses. Different types of searches have different purposes that are useful at different times in the inquiry process. Students often expect to conduct one comprehensive search, with the unfortunate result that the exploration stage is rushed through without gaining sufficient ideas to formulate a focus, and the collection stage is bogged down by general material not pertinent to the focus of the inquiry. In Guided Inquiry students gain a clear understanding of different types of searches to accomplish the tasks of the different stages of the inquiry process. Students are introduced to four types of searches: *preliminary*, *exploratory*, *comprehensive,* and *summary*. They learn to combine and adapt these to their own inquiry needs. The concept of different types of searches for accomplishing different objectives in the inquiry process is important for information literacy.

A *preliminary* search is helpful in the very early stages of the inquiry process. In a preliminary search students gain an overview of the general topic and an estimation of the amount and type of material available. This information is then used to select the general area or topic of their inquiry.

The purpose of an *exploratory* search is to explore ideas to gain a better understanding of the general topic and to identify ways to focus the inquiry. In the exploratory search information is gathered to define and extend the topic and lead to a focused perspective.

A *comprehensive* search is useful after considerable background information has led to ideas about forming a focus. In the early stages of inquiry a comprehensive search tends to bog down students' thinking in detail that is overwhelming and confusing. A focused perspective formed through the exploratory search provides a "guiding idea" for the comprehensive search. The purpose of the comprehensive search is to collect specific, pertinent information on the focused perspective of the inquiry.

A *summary* search is conducted in the presentation stage at the close of the inquiry process, when students are preparing to share their learning. Its purpose is to recheck information for anything missing or that may have been overlooked.

Concepts for Evaluating

The purpose of evaluating sources of information is to select what will be most useful for accomplishing the task at hand. Although usefulness is the underlying criterion for evaluating and selecting a source, there are many ways to judge usefulness. Evaluation of sources has become increasingly difficult and complex because of the vast range of information, particularly online. Guided Inquiry introduces students to several criteria to apply for selecting useful sources for their inquiry: considering the format, structure, and characteristics of sources to help them make intelligent choices. (See Figure 6.3.) Using these criteria, students compare sources to determine which will be most useful for their inquiry task.

Concepts for Evaluating
• Evaluating formats for reading, listening, viewing, and experiencing
• Structure gives clues for evaluating sources
• Characteristics for evaluating sources—expertise, accuracy, currency, perspective, quality

Figure 6.3. Concepts for Evaluating.

Choosing Formats for Reading, Listening, Viewing, and Experiencing

A fundamental concept for evaluating sources is that information comes in a number of different formats. There are formats for reading, listening, viewing, and experiencing as well as multimedia formats that incorporate several or all of these The range of formats includes books, magazines, journals, newspapers, databases, Web sites, videos, objects, and people. A format may be thought of as a package or container for the information. Different formats accommodate different ways of knowing and modes for learning.

Students need to think about the whole range of formats in their search for information. Through Guided Inquiry they learn to consider the entire library as an information source with a variety of materials in different formats. They learn to take into account the many resources outside the school, in their local community and through the Internet. They learn to consider how each type of format might inform them about their topic and to evaluate what will be most useful for them at a particular point in the inquiry process.

Guided Inquiry employs the school library as a laboratory for learning about the many different formats of information for reading, listening, viewing, and experiencing. Students learn to approach a library search from a number of different points of access to locate information in different formats. They also learn to expand their inquiry through museums and experts as well as films and television, many of these digitized for online access. They learn to apply the format of materials as evaluation criteria for choosing materials that are most useful for their own inquiry learning.

Structure Offers Clues for Evaluating Information

Sources are structured in a variety of ways, and understanding these differences enables students to evaluate the usefulness of a source for their inquiry tasks. In Guided Inquiry the concept of different structures is learned and applied through examples such as parts of a book, construction of databases and Web sites, organization of reference sources, and variety of genres. Understanding of these basic structures of print materials is expanded to other formats, such as those in museums and various media. Learning the structure of a source provides students with ways to find relevant information in it as a means for evaluating its usefulness.

Evaluating a source by the way it is structured is an important concept that enables students to making intelligent choices in their information seeking and use. In Guided Inquiry young children are introduced to the concept of structure of sources through becoming acquainted with the parts of a book. This sets the foundation for learning the structure of the whole range of print materials, including periodicals and reference sources, as well as those available electronically, such as databases and Web sites.

Understanding the concept of structure also builds competence in using a whole range of sources. Many students limit their information use to a few familiar sources, overlooking excellent materials such as reference sources. In Guided Inquiry students learn that a reference source is referred to for specific information and is not intended to be read all the way through. They learn to use the structure of the reference source to locate, evaluate, and use information for their inquiry. Elementary school children learn about the structure of general reference sources and achieve competence at using general encyclopedias and dictionaries. They become acquainted with subject encyclopedias in science and social studies and other curriculum areas. Building on this foundation, middle school students find that reference sources are particularly useful in the early stages of inquiry, when they have little knowledge of their topic. Secondary school students can determine which reference source is best for gathering a certain type of information that fits the topic and stage of their inquiry.

Guided Inquiry uses different genres to enhance the learning experience. A variety of genres of literature are introduced throughout elementary school and applied to inquiry learning in middle and secondary school. The division of fiction and nonfiction is important but sometimes overemphasized. Through Guided Inquiry ideas and information are derived from fiction as well as expository texts. For example, historical fiction is an excellent way to bring life and reality to the events in a remote time period. The various types of fiction, including mystery, fantasy, science, historical, adventure, sports, realistic, and humorous, are used as prompts for further inquiry in informational materials. Other genres, such as poetry, essays, music, short stories, plays, films, letters, and interviews, as well as pictures and objects, are incorporated in the rich resource environment of inquiry learning.

Five Characteristics for Evaluating Sources

Sources of information have certain distinct characteristics that enable people to select those that are most useful for them. Guided Inquiry introduces students to five criteria for evaluating sources and judging the usefulness of information for their inquiry tasks: *expertise*, *accuracy*, *currency*, *perspective*, and *quality*.

Expertise is the knowledge of the author. Students at an early age can consider who the author is and what qualifications the author has. Guided Inquiry leads students to recognize experts on a subject and to notice sources that are credible, comprehensive, and complete. They are guided to materials they can understand in credible secondary sources that explain an expert's work when the original source may be too difficult to comprehend. Expertise is valued for its usefulness and relevance in the inquiry process.

Accuracy is the factual correctness and authenticity of a source. Students may be misled by misinformation, particularly in sources they find on the Web. With their limited prior knowledge of a topic, they may have difficulty spotting errors. Guided Inquiry leads students to question whether facts are correct and if the material is free from obvious errors. They learn to recognize whether sources are thorough, sound, and sufficiently detailed for their inquiry task.

Currency is the date of publication or presentation of the material. Many research topics require material from a specific time period. Students can make the mistake of searching in the wrong place for the wrong time period. In Guided Inquiry they learn to establish whether their topic is a present-day, ongoing issue that requires the latest, most up-to date information, or something that took place in the past. Students learn the sources for the most current information and how to find information on topics from the past.

Perspective is the point of view and outlook of the author. Students need to become aware of the difference between sources that present an opinion or position and those that are primarily factual. Guided Inquiry helps students recognize material presented with a particular frame of reference or slant and to learn when these sources are useful and when they are confusing and limiting. In this way they can respect an author's way of looking at something while being alert to bias that distorts facts and restricts fairness. Basic to information literacy is the ability to distinguish between a factual report and an opinion piece and to select wisely from a range of perspectives.

Quality is the value and merit of an information source. It implies excellence in the writing, composing, and presentation of material as well as its content. Quality material is clear and understandable. It is well written and articulate. It is organized in a purposeful way. Quality is a summation of the other four evaluation characteristics. Guided Inquiry helps students learn to recognize quality in both composition and content through familiarity with a variety of well-chosen materials in the library collection and selected outside sources.

These five concepts are at the very core of evaluating sources. In Guided Inquiry they are applied to the whole range of materials and resources for making judgments about what to use in inquiry. It is essential for students to know these concepts and to apply them throughout their inquiry learning. A person who can apply these concepts to evaluate sources in the vast information environment is truly information literate and educated for the information age.

Concepts for Using

Once a source has been located and evaluated for usefulness it is time to put it to use for learning through inquiry. Guided Inquiry develops students' ability to use a variety of sources for learning through a comprehensive program of concepts, strategies and techniques that enable them to find meaning and gain deep understanding. These include determining importance; forming a focus; deciding what is enough; managing inquiry by taking notes and recording references; interpreting facts and organizing ideas; and sharing with community of learners (see Figure 6.4).

Concepts for Using

- Determining importance, relevance, and pertinence
- Forming a focus
- Deciding what is enough
- Managing inquiry: taking notes, recording references
- Interpreting facts and organizing ideas
- Sharing with a community of learnersI

Figure 6.4. Concepts for Using.

Determining Importance: From Relevance to Pertinence

The ability to determine importance in an information source is essential for learning from a variety of sources and is a basic skill for information literacy. Many teachers have observed that their students have difficulty deciding what to choose as important from the informational texts they read. Even students who are proficient readers often have difficulty when it comes to finding meaning in expository texts (Keene and Zimmermann, 1997). In Guided Inquiry students learn to determine importance from information texts as well as fiction texts in the early grades through deep discussion of what they recall, summarize, paraphrase, and extend from their reading. They learn not to take everything from a text but to choose only those things that are important to them. This is the beginning of understanding how to use ideas to create something of their own, of utmost importance in avoiding blatant copying and plagiarizing. Determining importance is particularly significant as students move from learning to read to reading to learn. Older students learn to choose information by considering how it relates to their research task and to select and extract information that helps them to accomplish what they have set out to do. The model of the ISP shows that the early stages of the inquiry process call for finding information that is relevant to the general topic and the later stages require only information that is pertinent to the focus of the inquiry. Students come to recognize that determining what is important in a text changes from relevance to pertinence as the inquiry progresses. An important component of information literacy is the ability to select what is important in a vast information environment.

Forming a Focus

The stages of the ISP give students a sense of the sequence of tasks they need to accomplish, from initiating, to selecting, to exploring, to forming, to collecting, to presenting. One of the essential tasks in the inquiry process is forming a focus. The focus is formed from what the student has learned in the exploration stage. It may be a theme or a point of view or an aspect of the topic that is the creative formulation of the student. The focus is the turning point of the inquiry, which moves the student from seeking general information to seeking pertinent information on his or her particular perspective. It serves as a guiding idea for the collecting and presenting stages. Developing a focused perspective makes each student's inquiry a bit different. The best guard against copying and plagiarism is the students' clear understanding that inquiry is a creative process in which they will be constructing, learning, and creating their own products.

Guided Inquiry employs the full inquiry process in middle school and concentrates on forming a focus with students in their preadolescent and early adolescent years. Inquiry for younger children consists primarily of fact finding and reporting. While the instructional team encourages some interpretation of facts, the full inquiry process is developed and reinforced later, in middle school. In secondary school students apply the full inquiry process throughout the curriculum. They learn to clearly distinguish between a right answer and a point of view. They become proficient at analyzing and synthesizing information from a variety of sources to present their perspective on a problem, topic, or area of inquiry. The concept of forming a focus during the inquiry process enables them to gain control and proficiency in learning from a variety of sources of information.

Deciding What Is Enough

The concept of *enough* involves the deceptively simple question, "What is enough?" The question of what is enough may have seemed fairly straightforward when a person could gather all there was to know on a topic in a contained collection. It is quite a different matter in the present information environment. Understanding what is enough is essential for finding meaning in the vast information available. *Enough* relates to seeking meaning in a quantity of information by determining what one needs to know and by formulating a focus on which to build. Guided Inquiry helps students to judge for themselves when they have enough information to make sense. They learn to decide what is enough to accomplish the task at hand. Applying the concept of enough in each stage of the inquiry process, the instructional team guides students in determining what is enough to recognize an information need; what is enough to select a general topic; what is enough to explore for background and ideas; what is enough to form a focus; what is enough to define and extend the focus; what is enough to accomplish the task that prompted the information seeking; and what is enough to share what has been solved, learned, or created. Being able to decide what is enough is important for information literacy.

Managing Inquiry: Keeping Track Along the Way

Managing inquiry to keep track of ideas, information, and sources along the way requires techniques for taking notes and recording references. Guided Inquiry introduces and develops management techniques in elementary school that are extended, reinforced, and applied in middle and secondary school.

Note taking is an essential skill for gathering ideas and collecting information throughout the inquiry process. As students read, they need to record ideas and facts that they regard as important and plan to use. Many students have difficulty deciding exactly what to take down in their notes. They frequently either make the mistakes of attempting to write down everything or of taking sparse notations that are not useful when they refer back to them. Note taking requires a degree of abstracting, a skill students acquire as they mature. Introducing a systematic method of note taking is helpful. Some teachers recommend the use of cards; others prefer notebooks. In Guided Inquiry note taking is matched to the stages of the inquiry process, and journals are used for keeping track. Journals are introduced in the early stages of the inquiry process for jotting down thoughts about the topic and progress of the inquiry. The journal becomes a notebook for listing ideas during the exploration stage and for recording important information related to the focus in the collection stage. The journal may be in the form of a handwritten note book or a word processing computer file, or some combination of the two.

The computer is an excellent tool for keeping track of sources and for recording citations to references. However, a section of a handwritten journal can work just as well to keep a log of sources. Guided Inquiry introduces elementary students to the idea of identifying their sources of information by adding the question "Where do I find out" to their inquiry guidelines. By middle school, students are advised to keep detailed citations of all their references in each stage of the inquiry process. In the early stages, when they are browsing for ideas, students often think that they don't need to take down the citation of every source they use. Without a log of sources, they readily lose track of what sources they have used and have difficulty finding them again later when they want to go more deeply into some of the initial ideas they came across. Even though they are advised against making too detailed notes in the early stages, which may bog down their inquiry, they will need to make precise citations of all the sources they use. Techniques for note taking and recording references are essential for managing inquiry and using a variety of sources of information.

Interpreting Facts and Organizing Ideas

The objective of inquiry learning is not merely to collect facts but to reflect and interpret those facts to construct deep understanding. When students view their research projects as a fact collecting exercise, they miss the most important element of inquiry, the interpretation of the facts for learning. The research assignment itself is sometimes the source of the copying and plagiarism problem. When students view the object of inquiry as pursuing their own understanding, blatant copying rarely occurs.

Guided Inquiry develops basic inquiry abilities that help students interpret facts and organize ideas. Recall, summarizing, paraphrasing, and extending are introduced in the early grades to build competence in using information for learning. In middle and secondary school, students apply these abilities to interpreting facts and organizing ideas in their inquiry projects. Guided Inquiry provides ways for students to develop their ideas through the interpretation of the facts they collect. Students' journals/notebooks contain their determination of important information collected from the resources they have used. The instructional team employs intervention strategies that foster reflection on the facts students have selected as important through opportunities to collaborate, converse, continue, choose, chart, and compose. These six intervention strategies, discussed in detail in chapter 9, provide practical ways for interpreting facts and organizing ideas that lead to construction, learning, and getting ready to share that learning with their community of learners.

Sharing with a Community of Learners

Through Guided Inquiry the instructional team creates a community of learners in which students learn together and learn from each other. The audience for student inquiry is not only the teacher but the whole class. This is substantially different from a more traditional approach to research assignments, in which the student produces a product for the teacher to grade. In many instances students work on their own and the teacher is the only person who actually sees the finished product. In Guided Inquiry the student's product of inquiry is opened to the whole community: fellow students, the entire instructional team, and sometimes the whole school community. One of the important objectives of Guided Inquiry is to expand the knowledge base of all students through collaborating and sharing. Students learn about a wide range of aspects of the area of the curriculum from each member of the class. In this way a community of learners is created with each student contributing to the knowledge base, providing a forum for the development and exchange of ideas. The instructional team enables and guides this process for the utmost benefit of all students.

Guided Inquiry facilitates students learning from each other throughout the inquiry process by providing ongoing opportunities to collaborate. Sometimes students work in pairs, other times in small discussion groups, at other times alone, and sometimes with the entire class. These opportunities for working together provide a means for construction and learning. Students try out their ideas and obtain responses and suggestions from others in their community. They become aware of where they need to dig more and recognize further questions that need to be addressed. This group interaction fosters critical thinking that leads to deep learning.

In Guided Inquiry the community of learners provides an environment for inquiry learning through elementary and secondary school. In elementary school students are involved in asking questions, seeking to know more, and sharing discoveries with others. In middle school students explore ideas from various sources, integrating those ideas into their own thinking in preparation for forming a focused perspective that they can develop for sharing and applying. In secondary school the community of learners provides a forum for an exchange of ideas and active engagement in analyzing, synthesizing, drawing conclusions, and identifying further questions and problems. Developing and facilitating a community of learners is a primary goal of Guided Inquiry.

Information Literacy Through Guided Inquiry

This chapter has presented major concepts that underlie information literacy and how these are learned by students through Guided Inquiry, from the very youngest child in prekindergarten to the graduating senior in secondary school. At the beginning of the chapter we raised the question of the importance of information literacy. This chapter has shown that information literacy forms the basis of how people learn in the information environment of the 21st century. By combining the underlying concepts of information literacy with major subject area curriculum standards, Guided Inquiry prepares students for living and working in the technological information society.

Meeting Content Area Curricular Standards Through Guided Inquiry

My kids gained an entire grade level and I attribute that to the inquiry projects in the library.
—middle school teacher

Guided Inquiry is especially pertinent for modern schools because it integrates information literacy standards with content area standards. Chapter 6 described information literacy standards and concepts that are integral to the Guided Inquiry approach. This chapter presents content area standards that can be met through Guided Inquiry alongside information literacy concepts and skills.

There are limitless possibilities for meeting content area standards through Guided Inquiry, and the national standards reinforce that potential. The content of Guided Inquiry is drawn from many areas of the curriculum. In this chapter we consider the national standards of the core curricular areas of English language arts, mathematics, science, and social studies. The standards in each of these disciplines are in line with the principles underlying Guided Inquiry. These major fields are in agreement that students learn best by connecting new knowledge to what they already know and by engaging and motivating students through active learning. They stress and encourage a constructivist approach to teaching and learning that is central to Guided Inquiry.

Curriculum Area National Standards

National curriculum standards have been developed in many subject areas to establish instructional guidelines for schools across the country. Like the information literacy standards, developed jointly by the American Association of School Librarians (AASL) and the Association for Educational Communications and Technology (AECT), the national education organizations in each discipline have developed subject area curriculum standards, thoughtfully crafted by teachers and scholars specializing in each discipline. Each set of standards presents high expectations of achievement for students. Consideration has been given to learning within the discipline, ways of meeting curriculum objectives through the practice of teaching and learning. Guided Inquiry draws on the national standards as important benchmarks for student learning in current subject area curricula.

Schools are charged with preparing students for the workplace, citizenship, and everyday life in a rapidly changing information environment. Close examination of subject area standards reveals that the designers have given careful consideration to the nature of information in the 21st century. They have identified what students should know and be able to do within the discipline. The sheer volume of information, combined with its ever-changing nature, precludes requiring students to memorize large bodies of information. Of course there are times when memorization is important and necessary. However, for the most part these standards require students to examine the larger questions of the discipline rather than memorize bits of information. The majority of the standards are positioned to be accomplished within an inquiry approach.

Common Themes in National Standards

Examination of national standards in English language arts, mathematics, science, and social studies reveals some important commonalities. (See Figure 7.1.) First, a common thread is a reflection of best practice on teaching and learning. In each area a constructivist approach is stressed. Second, each area recognizes that with the information "explosion" there is too much information to learn it all. Third, each subject focuses on broad areas to help students gain a larger picture of the discipline through themes and big ideas. Fourth, all four standards recognize that a change of approach is needed for 21st-century schools. The standards reflect this change by encouraging meaningful instruction, through integration and problem solving.

Common Themes in Subject Area Standards
• A constructivist approach to teaching and learning
• Information explosion: too much to learn it all
• Focus on broad themes and big ideas
• Meaningful instruction through integration and problem solving

Figure 7.1. Common Themes in Subject Area Standards.

Guided Inquiry is unique in that it combines all of these important aspects of teaching and learning. This approach recognizes the need for a change in information age schools and works to achieve a solution by integrating information literacy standards and content learning. In Guided Inquiry students learn to locate, evaluate, and use information while learning the content of the subject area. Students learn to navigate information within a discipline. Guided Inquiry provides information skills essential for 21st-century subject learning.

A common theme among subject area curricula is to develop deep understanding as the major objective of learning. In each discipline there is an urgency to push for meaningful learning and a focus on making sense of big ideas related to the field. A large number of the standards in the four major disciplines are best accomplished through the organic and authentic means of teaching and learning that Guided Inquiry provides.

Choosing Standards for Guided Inquiry

One of the first tasks of the Guided Inquiry team is to select standards that can be best accomplished through an inquiry unit. It is a challenging task to plan for a well-balanced curriculum to accomplish the many objectives required in the standards. The national standards help in this endeavor by arranging objectives around comprehensive themes.

Most objectives in the national standards can be accomplished through an inquiry approach. The integrated, overlapping, holistic learning of Guided Inquiry can accomplish more over the course of a school year than attempting to address each standard on its own. But certain standards lend themselves to an inquiry approach more than others. Objectives that require extensive investigation and considerable reflection are best suited to inquiry learning. The team may find that not all objectives are best met through an inquiry approach and need not be forced into Guided Inquiry.

To most effectively achieve multiple objectives through Guided Inquiry, it is necessary to plan a variety of learning experiences for students. Over the course of a school year inquiry units should include different kinds of questions, lead to the use of a variety of sources, and require a variety of final projects. Extensive planning ensures a good balance of literacy skills practiced, information literacy concepts applied, and content area themes addressed during a school year and throughout a student's elementary and secondary education.

This chapter presents a description of curriculum standards in core disciplines of English language arts, mathematics, science, and social studies, with discussion of how these standards may be met through Guided Inquiry. There are natural integrating points at which subject areas complement and enlighten one another. In these cases integration between two or more subjects can accomplish goals in several curriculum areas in one inquiry unit. For example, social studies and mathematics standards encourage integration among subjects. In many instances science and mathematics objectives naturally enhance one another. Language arts objectives may be met through application within social studies and science content. There are many opportunities across curricular areas where integration is meaningful and worthwhile. In this chapter we bridge the different areas and consider ways that work together to add value to the learning in each area. However, there is also value in the Guided Inquiry unit that remains in one content area. Every Guided Inquiry unit adds the bonus of incorporating the often overlooked information literacy as the core. The following sections explain how the standards of each of the four core curriculum areas fit into a Guided Inquiry approach, beginning with English language arts.

National Standards for English Language Arts

Central to a unit of Guided Inquiry is the use of the language arts. Students use the language arts to ask questions, think through problems, locate and use information, as well as to report to others. There is a significant overlap between the process of Guided Inquiry and what students should know and be able to do according to the language arts standards.

The two major organizations focused on English language arts education, the National Council of Teachers of English (NCTE) and the International Reading Association (IRA), came together to create the "Standards for the English Language Arts." Information regarding these standards can be found at the two organization Web sites, www.ncte.org and www.reading.org.

The language arts standards stress the ability to use language for a variety of purposes: "A central goal of English is to ensure that students are able to use language to address their own needs as well as the needs of their families, their communities, and the greater society." In particular, they recommend a focus on "four purposes":

1. obtaining information,

2. literary expression,

3. learning and reflection, and

4. problem solving and application.

In a Guided Inquiry unit all types of texts and resources are used to investigate ideas, time periods, facts, and problems. The vast majority of texts we encounter after schooling are nonfiction, used to find information. Students need assistance in knowing how to read and interpret nonfiction as well as fiction. When thinking about the texts alone, the process of inquiry and investigating questions is mostly centered on nonfiction texts. As this list shows, literature is only one area on which we must focus. When we think of English classes, we often assume literature study, which is an important part of culture and language arts. We see great value in adding literary interpretation to a Guided Inquiry unit. Guided Inquiry is unique in that it includes fiction to set the stage for inquiry or provide a rich context from which the students can engage in an inquiry study.

Obtaining Information

The language arts standards state that "by learning to use many different media—traditional and non-traditional, print and non-print—to collect and convey information, students become aware of the range of possibilities available to them for communicating with others. Building on the information gathering and presentation skills that students use routinely in everyday life, teachers can strengthen students' abilities to perform more complex and challenging tasks to enhance learning in other curricula areas." This is precisely what the Guided Inquiry unit accomplishes. As discussed in chapter 6, Guided Inquiry takes this learning further by incorporating information literacy concepts throughout the process. Through the teaching of information literacy alongside language arts, students learn the much-needed processes of locating, evaluating, and using information while honing their language and communication skills.

Literary Expression

In this approach to Guided Inquiry we incorporate all forms of literature. Literary interpretation is applied to deepen students' understanding of the world. Guided Inquiry uses literature to set a rich context for learning, to provide vivid descriptions of time periods, events, places, and experiences that enhance informational learning. As discussed in chapter 3, students are grouped in inquiry circles, where they engage in intellectual conversations about sources of information for their inquiry. The Guided Inquiry team listens to students' ideas, encourages their connections, and models discussion techniques. Instruction is targeted to students' needs through flexible grouping, use of inquiry journals for reflection and documentation, and participation in thoughtful conversations. Guided Inquiry provides continuing opportunities for practicing and improving skills needed for literary expression and interpretation.

Learning and Reflection

Through Guided Inquiry students are provided time to reflect and learn through pursuing their own questions. The standards state that, "students who are encouraged to use their literacy skills to pursue their own interests and questions are likely to discover this potential" of language as a powerful instrument. Frequent opportunities to talk and write journals and small group discussion may be especially productive to develop a sense of their own resourcefulness and of the possibilities that language makes available to them, and are better able to set and work toward their own goals." Guided Inquiry has the capacity to show students this potential of language as they work together to investigate problems and questions. Furthermore, it incorporates the use of journals and small group discussion as core components to help students realize their own resourcefulness and actualize the possibilities of language in real life.

Problem Solving and Application

The premise of Guided Inquiry is to assist students in the process of problem solving and applying their understandings to new situations. A description of the standards states that in order "to respond to everyday situations and grapple with issues that concern them students must be able to use language and pose significant questions to become informed, to obtain and communicate information, and to think critically and creatively. . . . The challenge for teachers is to draw on students' real needs for language and use these as a platform for learning and strengthening of their competencies." This challenge is accomplished through a Guided Inquiry approach. In Guided Inquiry students are asking questions for real reasons, conversing to help one another think through a problem or approach, and using language to plan and present information to a greater audience.

Guided Inquiry aligns with the thinking of language arts professionals about what students need to know and be able to do in 21st-century schools. Examination of the 12 standards reveals overlapping compatibility with Guided Inquiry.

12 Language Arts Standards

1. Students read a wide range of print and nonprint texts to build an understanding of texts, of themselves, and of the culture of the United States and of the world; to acquire new information; to respond to the needs and demands of society and the workplace; and for personal fulfillment.

2. (Item 2 intentionally excluded.)

3. Students apply a wide range of strategies to comprehend, interpret, evaluate, and appreciate texts.

4. Students adjust their use of spoken, written, and visual language to communicate effectively with a variety of audiences and for different purposes.

5. Students employ a wide range of strategies as they write and use different writing process elements appropriately to communicate.

6. Students apply knowledge of language structure, language conventions, media techniques, figurative language, and genre to create, critique and discuss print and nonprint texts.

7.   Students conduct research on issues and interests by generating ideas and questions, and by posing problems. They gather, evaluate, and synthesize data from a variety of sources to communicate their discoveries in ways that suit their purpose and audience.

8.   Students use a variety of technological and informational resources to gather and synthesize information to create and communicate knowledge.

9.   Students develop an understanding and respect for diversity in language use, patterns, and dialects across cultures, ethnic groups, geographic regions, and social roles.

10.   (Item 10 intentionally excluded.)

11.   Students participate as knowledgeable, reflective, creative, and critical members of a variety of literacy communities.

12.   Students use spoken, written, and visual language to accomplish their own purposes.

Although the language arts committee on standards was not aware of Guided Inquiry at the time of writing these standards, they align with what students accomplish over the course of a Guided Inquiry unit. (Standards 2 and 10 have been excluded because standard 2 focuses on literature interpretation and standard 10 focuses on English as a Second Language students using their home language to develop competency in English. These could be accomplished through a Guided Inquiry unit, but neither would probably be the main function.) Ten out of the twelve standards are clearly aligned and are best accomplished through the instructional approach of Guided Inquiry.

These language arts professionals state that through every experience our language is growing and that, "the students will best develop their knowledge skills and competence through meaningful experiences and instruction that recognize purpose, form and content as inextricably interrelated." Guided Inquiry provides a meaningful experience through which students have multiple and various opportunities to practice their language skills and abilities through planning, researching, organizing, communicating with others, and sharing information.

National Mathematics Standards

The National Council of Teachers of Mathematics (NCTM) continually revises its national standards to ensure the highest quality and most up-to-date curricula. NCTM has reshaped this document over 10 years to come up with well-balanced, high standards. The NCTM standards are currently used widely in the United States and Canada. Information regarding these standards can be found at the organization Web site at www.nctm.org.

The mathematic standards are arranged in six learning principles and ten standards. NCTM is in accord with Guided Inquiry based on actively constructing new knowledge out of prior experience and new resources. One learning principle states: "Students must learn mathematics with understanding, actively building new knowledge from experience and prior knowledge." This aligns with a constructivist approach and is best taught through investigations and inquiry.

Although people often consider math to be mostly memorization of facts (computational fluency) and numeration, there is a major movement at the national level to incorporate the processes students go through when they attempt to solve mathematical problems. The national curriculum reflects this movement. Many standards are devoted to direct instruction and memorization, as they argue that, "without the ability to compute effectively, students' ability to solve complex and interesting problems is limited," but the vast majority are problem-solving skills and process-oriented concepts. At the youngest ages, prekindergarten through grade 2, the standards ask that children be able to understand situations that entail multiplication and division, such as equal groupings of objects and sharing equally. Understanding situations is a very different type of learning than knowing multiplication facts, and both need emphasis and instruction. The standards that focus on understanding concepts lend themselves to an inquiry approach.

Mathematical inquiry can be set aside and taught on its own. However, there are many connections between the mathematical and the science and social studies standards. Often mathematics is the means to understanding scientific problems. In social studies, when considering problems of population and planning, mathematics fits right in. An approach that considers larger problems that place mathematical skills in real-world circumstances have great value in learning concepts for deep understanding and using numeration skills in context.

The ten mathematical standards are described as having two larger goals. The first five are described as content area goals: numbers and operations, algebra, geometry, measurement, and data analysis and probability. The second five are described as goals for the process of problem solving: connections, communication, reasoning and proof (these are 3 and 4), and representation. All have their place in Guided Inquiry. The goals in boldface type are suited to inquiry learning.

The standards state: "Instructional programs from pre-kindergarten through grade 12 should enable all students to" do what is discussed in each category below.

Numbers and Operations

- **Understand numbers, ways of representing numbers, relationships among numbers, and number systems**

- **Understand meanings of operations and how they relate to one another**

- Compute fluently and make reasonable estimates

Algebra

- **Understand patterns, relations, and functions**

- Represent and analyze mathematical situations and structures using algebraic symbols

- Use mathematical models to represent and understand quantitative relationships

- **Analyze change in various contexts**

Geometry

- **Analyze characteristics and properties of two- and three-dimensional geometric shapes and develop mathematical arguments about geometric relationships**

- **Specify locations and describe spatial relationships using coordinate geometry and other representational systems**

- **Apply transformations and use symmetry to analyze mathematical situations**

- **Use visualization, spatial reasoning, and geometric modeling to solve problems**

Measurement

- **Understand measurable attributes of objects and the units, systems, and processes of measurement**

- **Apply appropriate techniques, tools, and formulas to determine measurements**

Data Analysis and Probability

- **Formulate questions that can be addressed with data and collect, organize, and display relevant data to answer them**

- **Select and use appropriate statistical methods to analyze data**

- **Develop and evaluate inferences and predictions that are based on data**

- **Understand and apply basic concepts of probability**

Problem Solving

- **Build new mathematical knowledge through problem solving**

- **Solve problems that arise in mathematics and in other contexts**

- **Apply and adapt a variety of appropriate strategies to solve problems**

- **Monitor and reflect on the process of mathematical problem solving**

In each of the first five areas, most goals can be taught through an inquiry approach. When students are asked to solve problems and apply strategies, these are best accomplished in the rich contextual setting provided in Guided Inquiry. For example, a class has read articles about a town issue that is being debated. The town has acquired some land and is publicly debating what to do with it. The two proposals are a skate park and an affordable housing development. The housing could earn money for the town, and the park could as well. But which would be better for the town? How much money could each bring in? How much would each cost to build? How many apartments could be built according to local code for that space? This problem, considering the town's restraints and guidelines, would give the students an actual situation to think about while considering social, ecological, and practical implications of this math problem.

The cost and possible profit of the intended uses of this land is a real problem for students to engage in. Once they have their statistics straight, they can create a proposal and make an informed decision to present at a town board meeting. This is the type of rich context that Guided Inquiry affords for applying mathematical skills.

The second five standards are even more related to inquiry, as they are all related to the process of problem solving. Again, the standards in boldface type are specifically well suited to inquiry.

Connections

- Recognize and use connections among mathematical ideas

- Understand how mathematical ideas interconnect and build on one another to produce a coherent whole

- **Recognize and apply mathematics in contexts outside of mathematics**

Communication

- **Organize and consolidate their mathematical thinking through communication**

- **Communicate their mathematical thinking coherently and clearly to peers, teachers, and others**

- **Analyze and evaluate the mathematical thinking and strategies of others**

- **Use the language of mathematics to express mathematical ideas precisely**

Reasoning and Proof

- Recognize reasoning and proof as fundamental aspects of mathematics

- **Make and investigate mathematical conjectures**

- **Develop and evaluate mathematical arguments and proofs**

- **Select and use various types of reasoning and methods of proof**

Representation

- **Create and use representations to organize, record, and communicate mathematical ideas**

- **Select, apply, and translate among mathematical representations to solve problems**

- **Use representations to model and interpret physical, social, and mathematical phenomena**

These areas require inquiry and are based on processes rather than learning specific number skills. Communicating ideas about math and the process that students go through to complete a problem, as well as drawing connections to other content areas such as science and social studies, can all be woven into a Guided Inquiry unit. Representations allow students to recognize connections and communicate them to others. Presenting an argument or scientific idea with the mathematical proof behind is a process provided in an inquiry unit.

Math lends itself to an integrative approach as well as an inquiry approach. Mathematical goals and standards are best addressed in the rich context of guided inquiry. As NCTM recognizes, often mathematics is most relevant when considering questions from other content areas such as science or social studies.

National Science Standards

The National Science Teachers Association (NSTA) created the national science standards. Information regarding these standards can be found at the organization's Web site at www.nsta.org. When considering what students should know and be able to do, science teachers had a major problem to contend with. For many years they attempted to present the minutia of scientific facts and organized them so that the curriculum would build over the years of schooling. In recent years the NSTA has come to a new conclusion. Scientific knowledge is continually changing as scientific advances are made. This makes it difficult to keep the science curriculum current. With this realization, NSTA adjusted its approach to teaching science that shaped the standards and expectations for prekindergarten to grade 12 education.

A new approach is reflected in the standards and is in line with what the information science community has been reporting about the vast and growing amount of information available. There is a new emphasis on inquiry in the current *National Science Education Standards*. The new version of the standards reflects the notion that "though the content of science may change and develop over time the conceptual organization of science will remain the same and what is needed is to provide students with the knowledge, understanding and abilities that will improve their scientific literacy."

The standards specifically stress a reduction of learning facts in the content areas of science and more emphasis on process, inquiry, deep understanding, and communicating ideas. NSTA suggests the study of fundamental concepts. Rather than covering material in a class period or two, they suggest extended investigations to promote deep understanding.

The organization states that, "Students' understandings and abilities are grounded in the experiences of inquiry, and inquiry is the foundation for the development of understandings and abilities of the other content areas." NSTA encourages a "multidisciplinary" approach and "providing many opportunities for integrated approaches to science teaching."

NSTA sets out eight categories of content standards:

Unifying concepts and processes in science

Science as inquiry

Physical science

Life science

Earth and space science

Science and technology

Science in personal and social perspectives

History and nature of science

The eight categories are a well-rounded perspective on what science is today. Each area helps students to understand science as a field as well as "how to do science." For example, "science as inquiry" is an equal standard to each of the domains of science. In keeping with the new approach, students are expected to understand what science is and what scientists do, as well as the history of science and social perspectives on scientific advances.

Unifying Concepts and Processes

This category includes the big picture of science topics and the major schemes through which all science can be understood:

> Systems, order, and organization

> Evidence, models, and exploration

> Change, constancy, and measurement

> Evolution and equilibrium

> Form and function

These "integrative schemes" provide natural application for Guided Inquiry. Each could be the theme of a unit of its own, or they could be considered the larger lens through which the students make a closer inspection of another topic. Considering science as related to these larger themes sets the curriculum up for inquiry as it presents ideas in the form of schemes through which many topics in science can be understood.

Science as Inquiry

NSTA views inquiry as "basic" to science education, stressing that teachers focus on conducting inquiries and developing understanding. They recommend that teachers provide students with opportunities to "think and act in ways associated with inquiry, asking questions, planning and conducting investigations, using appropriate tools and techniques to gather data, thinking critically and logically about relationships between evidence and explanations, constructing and analyzing alternative explanations." Guided Inquiry is precisely this process. When students investigate a science theme or problem through Guided Inquiry, they are involved in all of these activities.

Physical, Life, and Earth and Space Sciences

Physical, life, and earth and space are the "widely accepted divisions of the domain of science." In these areas the standards focus on the facts, concepts, principles, theories, and models that are important for all students to know, understand, and be able to use. This is a general overview of the K–12 standards and does not show the breakdown of area by grade level. An examination of the standards reveals what can be taught through an inquiry approach.

Within the domains of science, characteristics, properties, structures, and functions can be studied through an inquiry approach. Inquiry can begin with a larger question and move forward into a specific investigation to understand that question in even more detail. Each of the standards listed here can be accomplished through an inquiry approach.

Physical Science
- Properties and structures of matter
    - Chemical reactions
- Properties of motion and forces
- Energy
    - Transfer and conservation of
    - Interactions with matter

Life Science

- Characteristics, structures and functions of organisms, living systems, and the cell
- Lifecycles, heredity, and biological evolution
- Interdependence of organisms
- Populations and ecosystems
- Matter, energy, and organization in living systems
- Organisms and environment
    - Diversity and adaptations of organisms
    - Behavior of organisms

Earth and Space Science

- Properties of earth materials
- Structures of the earth system and energy in the earth system
- Objects in the sky, earth's history, geochemical cycles
- Changes in earth and sky, earth in the solar system, origin and evolution of the earth system
- Origin of the universe

Science and Technology

Science and technology includes the process of design and investigates how science is linked with technology. These are the main topics related to this category:

- Difference between natural objects and human-made objects
- Abilities of technological design
- Understanding of technology and science

These complement the "science as inquiry" standard. They call for "students to identify and state a problem, including a cost and risk and benefit analysis, design and implement a solution and evaluate the solution." These tasks are a part of the inquiry process and call for Guided Inquiry. In addition, science and technology directly relates to mathematics as well as economics and is a natural area in which integration of subjects can enhance understanding.

Science in Personal and Social Perspectives

This area of the standards is especially designed to help students develop decision-making skills related to what they "will face as citizens in today's society." These could be termed current issues in science and offer multiple possibilities for inquiry learning:

- Personal and community health
- Population growth (resources and environment)
- Resources, natural and other
- Environmental quality
- Risks and benefits

- Natural and human-induced hazards
- Science and technology in local, national, and global challenges

These social perspectives on science offer a wide range of possibilities for questions that students have about the scientific advances that relate to their daily lives. These areas naturally connect with the social studies and offer an opportunity for collaboration between these subjects. Through Guided Inquiry students can engage in meaningful and powerful investigations in this area of science that connects with their lives.

History and Nature of Science

NSTA agrees that students must come to understand science as a human endeavor that reflects history and is an ongoing and changing enterprise. This area of the standards lends itself to Guided Inquiry. For example, an inquiry unit may begin with historical fiction and work its way into the investigation of science as a human endeavor that is changing and ever evolving. The history of science lends itself to integration with social studies and history curriculum.

In general, most science standards can be met through Guided Inquiry. There are also multiple opportunities to collaborate across subject areas within the science standards.

National Social Studies Standards

The National Council for the Social Studies (NCSS) created the social studies standards. These can be found at www.ncss.org. Just as in the other disciplines, the social studies committee considered principles for teaching and learning to guide instruction in its area. NCSS breaks down the discipline into ten major themes on which performance objectives are based.

First the committee puts forth principles for teaching and learning. These principles align with Guided Inquiry as described in this book. They state that social studies teaching and learning are powerful when they are

> meaningful,
>
> integrated,
>
> value based,
>
> challenging, and
>
> active.

Guided Inquiry is powerful and meaningful under this definition of teaching and learning. Inquiry learning relates to real questions and the students' lives as well as the content of the curriculum. Guided Inquiry is integrated. Through a Guided Inquiry unit students are engaging in information literacy, language arts, and content area questions. Through inquiry students come across the "values, complexities, and dilemmas involved in an issue." By using many different types of sources as well as engaging in conversation with their peers, students see varying positions and opposing points of view. Guided Inquiry is challenging. Students integrate what they know about their world and what information they gather to create a new and interesting perspective to share with others. Students are engaged in reflective thinking and decision making throughout Guided Inquiry as they narrow their focus, collaborate with others, gather and interpret information, and create a method of sharing. In these ways Guided Inquiry provides a powerful context for social studies learning.

Ten Themes of the Social Studies Standards

Social studies professionals recognize the need for a new type of learning in 21st-century schools. They present these broad themes to guide instruction and enable teachers to make decisions about how and what to teach their students. They see the themes as "organizing strands for social studies curriculum at every school level." Social studies programs should include experiences that provide for the study of

1. culture and cultural diversity;
2. the way human beings view themselves in and over time;
3. people, places, and environments;
4. individual development and identity;
5. interactions among individuals, groups, and institutions;
6. how people create and change structures of power, authority, and governance;
7. how people organize the production, distribution, and consumption of goods and services;
8. relationships among science, technology, and society;
9. global connections and interdependence; and
10. the ideals, principles, and practices of citizenship in a democratic republic.

In the description of each of these standards, NCSS has set out questions that might be answered through investigation. These questions are often appropriate for inquiry learning and are included in the following discussion of the standards with regard to Guided Inquiry.

Culture and Cultural Diversity

Culture and cultural diversity are important for students from a multicultural society to understand. It is also important to include multiple perspectives that "derive from different cultural vantage points." An inquiry learning focused in this theme investigates questions like these: "What are the common characteristics of different cultures? How does culture change to accommodate different ideas and beliefs? What does language tell us about culture?" Through a study of culture, students explore topics of geography, history, and anthropology, as well as sociology. These types of questions and others are good examples of an introduction to a Guided Inquiry unit.

Time, Continuity, and Change: The Way Human Beings View Themselves in and over Time

Through this theme students consider and develop a historical perspective on problems and events. Inquiry learning focused on this theme investigates questions such as these: "What happened in the past? How am I connected to those in the past? How has the world changed and how might it change in the future? How can the perspective we have about our own life experiences be viewed as a part of the larger human story across time?" This theme is ripe with possibilities for investigations into the past, examining relationships, points of view, and events.

People, Places, and Environments

This theme entails the whole of geography. Considering the world under this lens, students can think with a geographic perspective. Inquiry learning focusing on this theme investigates questions such as these: "Where are things located? Why are they located where they are? What patterns are reflected in the location of things? How do landforms change? What implications do these have for people?" This area of study helps learners make informed decisions about relationships between human beings and the environment. These types of questions fit well with an inquiry approach.

Individual Identity and Development

While studying identity and how people form identities, an examination of the influence of culture, institutions, and groups is necessary. Students consider some of these questions: "What influences how people learn, perceive and grow? How do people meet their basic needs in a variety of contexts?" The nature of this theme and most other of the social studies standards is that they overlap with other standards. In considering identity, students will come across institutional, cultural, and group influences on people. In this way the social studies standards are overlapping and well suited to inquiry learning.

Interactions Among Individuals, Groups, and Institutions

This standard integrates areas of psychology, sociology, anthropology, political science, and history. Under this standard, students may ask questions such as: "What is the role of institutions in this and other societies? How do institutions change? What is my role in institutional change?" These are important questions in a democratic society. An example from the early grades in the social studies standards explains how students examine and observe ant and bee colonies and compare them to human societies. Older students might investigate particular individuals of the past to examine how they shaped a specific time period through political, economic, or cultural means.

How People Create and Change Structures of Power, Authority, and Governance

Questions that arise from this standard include "What is power? What forms does it take? Who holds it? How is it gained, used and justified? What is legitimate authority? How are governments created, structured, maintained and changed? How can we keep government responsive to its citizens' needs and interests? How can individuals' rights be protected within the context of majority rule?" In this area the students are dealing with government, politics, political science, history, and law, among other social sciences. Younger students can create a mock community to investigate the need for rules and laws as well as how to enforce them. Older students could examine the paths to independence taken by different countries. High school students might consider the amendments to the U.S. Constitution or political cartoons.

How People Organize the Production, Distribution, and Consumption of Goods and Services

"What is produced? How is production to be organized? How are goods and services distributed? What is the most effective allocation of the factors of production land, labor, capital, and management?" These are excellent questions when considering the theme of economics. In a capitalist society these are important areas to be knowledgeable and informed about. Through inquiry into this standard students would expand their understanding of economics as it relates to their own lives and their world. For example, they might examine the different gas price hikes to consider causes and effects. Students could create an assembly line and examine supply, demand, labor, creativity, independence, and quality control issues. Students could examine the historical perspective of an event, such as how wartime affected the economy during that period.

Relationships Among Science, Technology, and Society

This standard directly overlaps with the science standard of "science and technology" but has a social emphasis. Inquiry learning focused in this theme investigates questions such as these: "Is new technology always better than that which it will replace? What can we learn from past about how new technologies will result in social change, some of which is unanticipated? How can we cope with an ever-increasing pace of change? How can we manage technology so that the greatest number of people benefit from it? How can we preserve our fundamental values and beliefs in a world that is rapidly becoming one technology-linked village?" In this theme the emphasis is on the social implications of technology. This could easily be paired with a science unit on technology, with one group of students examining social implications while another considers the same topic from a scientific perspective. The implications of technology for the past and present world are well suited to inquiry learning.

Global Connections and Interdependence

Although the committee did not include questions about this standard, consider the following: "How do language, arts, music, belief systems and other cultural elements facilitate understanding or misunderstanding? How are we as a nation economically dependent on other nations? What are the basic human rights? What role should we play in guaranteeing that all people have basic human rights? How are we locally connected to the greater global community? How do our own stereotypes play into our understanding of the world? What are global issues, and how do we address them?" These are only a few of the many questions that fall under this standard and are well matched with an inquiry approach.

The Ideals, Principles, and Practices of Citizenship in a Democratic Republic

Living in a democratic society, it is always important for citizens to understand their roles in society. Through this standard students might investigate these questions: "What is civic participation? How can I be involved? How has the meaning for citizenship evolved? What is the balance of rights and responsibilities? What is the role of a citizen in the community and the nation, and as a member of the world community? How can I make a positive difference?" Maybe even more pertinent to students is why they should get involved and what good it would do. Giving students opportunities to act on their questions and get involved is a part of Guided

Inquiry. When investigating real-world problems, students become motivated to do something about them. Through Guided Inquiry they are encouraged and guided to know what might make the greatest impact and be appropriate for them to do to get involved as citizens in our country. The final project takes many shapes and forms, and many include becoming a part of the solution to a problem.

The social studies themes and standards are aligned with an inquiry approach. Each area, as explained by the standards committee, is open ended and well matched with an inquiry approach. The examples and questions provided here are only the "tip of the iceberg" when it comes to the possibilities of inquiry learning. Often social studies teachers engage their students in inquiry learning. However, many times the projects are built around the academic task of creating a research paper. The Guided Inquiry approach creates a rich learning context around which the projects take on more meaning and build intrigue as students investigate their own wonderings about topics. Guided Inquiry raises the bar on the traditional approach to teaching social studies and is aligned with the standards.

Students Meeting Standards

It is necessary to track each student's learning. If students are working in small inquiry circles, how does the instructional team know what each student is learning? There are many aspects of the Guided Inquiry approach presented in this book that help the instructional team to track and assist students' learning. Holding conferences and teaching through interventions are discussed in depth in chapter 9. Products like charts and journals, which students create to help them gather and synthesize information along their path, are tools to see into the mind's eye of the student. When paired with a conference with the instructional team, these tools are a powerful resource for assessing student content area learning. Of course the final presentation, in whatever form, is a useful artifact to examine, but it should not be taken as the sole testament to what each student has learned over the course of the unit. Assessment during the inquiry process is equally as important for knowing what students are learning as the evaluation of the final product. Chapter 8 is devoted to assessment in Guided Inquiry.

This examination of the four major national standards reveals that there is great promise in what students should know and be able to do. These standards pave the way for implementing Guided Inquiry. In most cases, the national standards lend themselves directly to this style of teaching.

Assessment in Guided Inquiry

Students improved their skills in critical thinking and information seeking and this could be demonstrated on the SLIM.
—high school librarian

Guided Inquiry is an active process for both students and instructors. It is based on continual assessment and evaluation throughout an inquiry unit. Assessment and evaluation inform the instructional team about when students need intervention and what intervention is required, as well as what students have learned.

An important difference between assessment and evaluation is the formative function of assessment and the summary function of evaluation. Assessment throughout the inquiry process alerts the team to what students have already learned and what requires further intervention and teaching as the inquiry unit progresses. Evaluation at the end of the inquiry unit indicates what students have learned and achieved throughout the entire unit.

Evaluation of a research assignment traditionally has been the teacher's grade of the research paper. A grade on a paper is a limited indication of the specific learning that has taken place in the inquiry. Evaluation of the end product rarely identifies specific weaknesses and strengths in the inquiry process of students. This type of evaluation provides limited opportunity for the students to reflect on the process and develop their own growth potential.

The call for authentic assessment grew alongside the standardized testing movement in the latter part of the 20th century as the need for assessing student learning became urgent. Since 2000 there has been a noticeable increase in emphasis on assessment in school library literature. Harada and Yoshina (2004) have been leaders in addressing assessment for inquiry learning. They have included practical assessment strategies for each stage of inquiry in planning for elementary, middle, and high school students. They focus on four core fundamentals related to assessment:

- Assessment is a critical tool to help students determine their strengths and weaknesses and work on improvements.

- Assessment is an equally valuable means of analyzing and informing instruction.

- Assessment is not evaluation; it is infused throughout the learning and teaching experience rather than limited to final outcomes.

111

- Assessment is not an add-on; it is integral to effective teaching and learning. (Harada and Yoshina, 2005)

Although it is important to be able to evaluate what students have learned at the end of an inquiry unit, even more important for Guided Inquiry is consideration of formative assessment along the way. Guided Inquiry depends on following progress throughout the unit and modeling, guiding, and instructing at critical zones of intervention. The instructional team plans for assessment throughout the inquiry process to identify students' evolving needs and adjusts the plan accordingly to ensure that students are receiving guidance and instruction for deep learning.

Guided Inquiry is based on formative assessments that provide students with prompt feedback and timely intervention during the inquiry unit as an important component of the learning process. Assessment methods, such as conferences, observation, and student journals, indicate what has been learned and what hasn't. The information gathered in these settings indicates what intervention is necessary and timely for each student at the various stages of the inquiry process. These types of assessments enable all members of the instructional team to make informed decisions for guiding and instructing students. The purpose of assessment is to identify what learning has taken place and where students need guidance, advice, and instruction.

Complexity of Assessing Inquiry Learning

In previous chapters we discussed the complexity of inquiry learning, with many kinds of learning going on at the same time. Students are involved simultaneously in learning about curriculum content, information literacy, the learning process, literacy ability, and social interaction. They are locating sources of information and choosing what is useful, relevant, and pertinent for their project. At the same time they are experiencing the process of learning from the information in these sources that is described in the model of the ISP. They are learning content from the sources and developing subject area knowledge. They are also developing literacy skills by comprehending what they are reading, articulating what they are thinking, and writing about their learning. In addition, they are involved in social interaction in small groups, work pairs, and the whole group. Each of these different types of learning requires assessment. It is important to be clear which aspect of learning you are seeking to assess. Some methods collect data on more than one type of learning, but there is unlikely to be one technique that addresses all five types of learning the student is experiencing. (See Figure 8.1.) It is important to be aware of what learning is assessed by any particular method and be guided accordingly.

Five Kinds of Learning in the Inquiry Process	
1. Curriculum content	fact finding, interpreting, and synthesizing
2. Information literacy	concepts for locating, evaluating, and using
3. Learning how to learn	initiating, selecting, exploring, focusing, collecting, and presenting
4. Literacy competence	reading, writing, speaking, and listening
5. Social skills	interacting, cooperating, and collaborating

Figure 8.1. Five Kinds of Learning in the Inquiry Process.

An important advantage of inquiry learning is that many things are being learned at the same time. The complexity of the learning environment is more like the outside world and more authentic to the student's experience, more interesting and engaging. This complexity also makes assessment more difficult, but not impossible. With thoughtful planning and a keen awareness of the students' experience, the Guided Inquiry team can adopt assessment techniques that provide data on the different kinds of learning in an inquiry unit. Assessment indicates zones of intervention for each kind of learning that the student is experiencing.

Research on Assessment of Learning in School Libraries

The Center for International Scholarship in School Libraries (CISSL) at Rutgers University has conducted a number of studies on the impact of school libraries on student learning. In one study, more than 13,000 students in grades 3–12 in Ohio schools responded to electronic surveys about how libraries help them to learn (Todd and Kuhlthau, 2005a, 2005b); 99.4 percent responded that the school library helped them to learn better. Nine help constructs were identified from the students' responses. According to the students, the school library

- saves me time with doing my school work;
- enables me to complete my work on time;
- helps me by providing a study environment for me to work;
- helps me take stress out of learning,
- helps me know my strengths and weaknesses with information use,
- helps me do work more effectively,
- provides me with a safe environment for ideas investigation, and
- helps me set my goals and plans.

These same studies reveal that effective school libraries with qualified school librarians have been having an impact on student learning for many years. But what is going on in school libraries that is making a difference for students? What are some of the indicators that show students are learning? How do librarians and teachers assess learning in school libraries? What are some methods for evaluating and assessing learning that have implications for designing Guided Inquiry? This chapter considers these questions within the framework of Guided Inquiry.

Research on Librarians' Assessment of Student Learning

In the mid-1990s a three-year evaluation of the National Library Power initiative was conducted to improve school libraries in major urban centers across the United States. One of the key questions addressed was, "Has Library Power influenced student learning opportunities?" The school librarians' descriptions of student learning within this national school improvement program provided an opportunity to gain insight into what criteria librarians used to assess learning.

The National Library Power Program, funded by the DeWitt-Wallace Reader's Digest Fund, sought to improve opportunities for student learning by upgrading school libraries in 19 urban communities. The program provided grants to public schools over a three-year period to improve teaching and learning through better and innovative uses of enhanced, up-to-date libraries. Grants of $1.2 million to each of the participating communities were used to renovate library space; purchase new books and upgrade print and electronic collections; and provide professional development to librarians, teachers, and principals to learn how to work together to make the best use of their new libraries. In return, each school had to commit to hiring and paying the salaries of full-time certified school librarians; keeping the library open and accessible to everyone throughout the school day; and increasing spending for books, software, and educational materials (Hopkins and Zweizig, 1999).

A study of librarians' perceptions of student learning was conducted within the evaluation of this national school improvement project (Kuhlthau, 1999d). One of the items on the annual Library Power evaluation survey of librarians was designed to elicit perceptions of student learning. Librarians were asked to respond to the following prompt: "Think back over your Library Power Program to when a student or students had a meaningful learning experience in the library. How did you know something new was learned? What stands out in your mind that made it a good learning experience?"

The librarians' responses provided critical incidents that were considered to typify what first comes to mind when a librarian is asked to describe student learning. The responses were coded on a 5-point scale of what the librarians emphasized as an indication of student learning. Responses that emphasized the librarian's actions and not what the students did, such as adding to the collection or describing a lesson taught, were coded as Input. Responses that emphasized quantitative measures of student use, such as a greater number of materials circulated, more class visits, or increased technology use, were coded as Output. Responses that emphasized a change in student attitude, such as increased interest and enthusiasm, were coded as Attitude. Responses that emphasized library and information skills, such as ability to locate materials or ability to use an online encyclopedia, were coded as Skills. Responses that emphasized content learning, such as using resources to learn about a subject in the curriculum, were coded as Utilization. (See Figure 8.2.)

Librarian Responses on Student Learning	
Input	resources and instruction
Output	amount of student library use
Attitude	change in student attitude
Skills	search skills and technology use
Utilization	information use for content learning

Figure 8.2. Librarian Responses on Student Learning.

In each of the three years, the combined levels of attitude, skills, and utilization represented approximately 85 percent of what the librarians emphasized in their responses. Comparison of the responses in each of the three years, however, showed important changes. Over the course of the Library Power initiative many librarians had changed their emphasis on what they considered important to describe about student learning. Early in the initiative they noted a change in attitude. Next they stressed competence in locating information and using technology. In the final year of the study many had turned their attention to using information for learning in the content areas of the curriculum. This progression showed that, over time, fully functioning libraries with qualified school librarians were influencing students' opportunities to learn, at least from the librarians' perspective. By the end of the three-year study many of the librarians' descriptions of student learning emphasized using information to achieve the overall objectives of the curriculum of the school.

This study of changes in librarians' thinking about assessment of student learning during the three years of the Library Power initiative provided insight into the state of assessment at the close of the 20th century. Over the three years of the initiative, the librarians became more involved in collaborative planning and teaming in the content areas of the curriculum through professional development and through their day-to-day experiences in the schools. There is some evidence of a gradual shift to inquiry learning over time. Librarians were able to focus on more meaningful aspects of student learning over the course of the Library Power initiative. In other words, the most effective school libraries were not just used as places to learn about library skills, but library skills were being used in the service of learning throughout the curriculum.

Indicators of Learning

A further analysis was made of the librarians' responses to identify some indicators of learning that the librarians were applying as criteria to assess student learning. Indicators of learning were identified in over 60 percent of the librarians' responses. The librarians' indicators of learning were organized into three tiers: observation, the first tier; performance, the second tier; and products and tests, the third tier. Figure 8.3 depicts the three tiers of indicators of learning in the order in which there were identified in the librarians' responses.

Indicators of Learning as Applied by Librarians		
Tiers of Observations	Observed Indicators of Learning	Responses (%)
First Tier: Casual Observation	• Comes back again	14.7
	• Positive comments	12.7
	• Expression on faces	12.0
Second Tier: Student Performance	• Shows independence in applying skills	19.9
	• Helps other students	9.2
	• Shares ideas with others	8.0
	• Asks questions; makes connections	8.0
	• Recalls later	6.4
Third Tier: Products and Tests	• Final products	6.8
	• Test results	2.4
		100.0

Figure 8.3. Indicators of Learning as Applied by Librarians.

The results of this analysis identified ten indicators of learning that ranged from casual observation to documented evidence. One way of assessing learning in libraries is to observe students while they are using the library, typical of the first tier 40 percent of the responses. The librarians observed that students came back to the library and made positive comments to the library staff, and that their facial expressions showed that they were learning.

The second tier of responses represents more interaction and involvement on the part of students, with emphasis on content learning and information literacy. More interactive, content-related indicators were mentioned in 50 percent of the librarians' responses. This reveals the librarians' awareness of using student performance as an indication of learning rather than just general observation. The librarians responded that students were independent in applying skills; helped other students; shared their ideas with other students, teachers, and librarians; asked questions; and made connections. The teachers also tracked learning by listening to what the students recalled about their learning some time later.

The librarians' observations went deeper to examine what students were doing. Ninety percent of their assessments included observations of attitude and performance. Documenting substantial effects of learning mentioned in the third tier of indicators represented less than 10 percent of responses by the librarians. A few librarians responded that they used final products and tests to reveal student learning.

Methods for Assessing Inquiry Learning

The librarians in the Library Power program identified observation and performance as the main ways of determining that students are learning. However, the librarians gave no indication that they were employing any instruments or particular methods for gathering evidence to assess learning using observation and performance. The Guided Inquiry team will need to plan for specific assessment methods that document their observations and students' performance for identifying progress and problems.

The best assessment methods are embedded in the inquiry process and are not cumbersome or intrusive. Assessment should be part of the students' own learning process. Wherever possible assessment should be folded into the inquiry task. Many of the methods of intervention discussed in chapter 9 may also be adopted as assessment tools.

Methods for documenting evidence of students' learning through observation, performance, and end product and tests are discussed in the next section. These methods serve a wide range of assessment functions by revealing different aspects of students' learning. When taken together these assessment methods provide essential information for the instructional team for guiding student inquiry.

Observation

Observation was identified by the Library Power librarians as an important way to identify learning. These casual observations were informative. The librarians made general observations of library use, students' attitudes, and students' comments. They informally judged learning by noting that students come back and make positive comments, and by the expression on their faces. This casual approach to observation can be made more effective by documenting the observations.

A useful method to document observations is keeping a written record at the time or shortly afterward. Members of the instructional team record their observations, particularly noting when a student or a group of students are struggling or when an important question has been raised or a connection made. The recorded observations become a valuable assessment tool by using timely documentation, in what researchers call, "field notes." These records are then discussed and analyzed with the rest of the team members to guide the ongoing inquiry.

Records of conferences and observations of students' inquiry process provide valuable information on student learning. These become part of each team member's daily routine. Each member of the instructional team makes a diligent effort to continually check in with students, make notes about their progress, and analyze notes for indication of patterns. The instructional team should communicate frequently with one another about their observations of student learning over the course of the unit. What occurs with one group in a conference may not be replicated at another time. When an observation is made by one member of the instructional team, it is important to make note of it and share that information with the other team members.

Field notes are extremely important. If notes are not taken and the team relies on mental notes, these will be difficult to re-create at a later time. It is important for all team members to keep track of and share with one another their observations of what use students are making of information they gather, what choices they are making, and what ideas and constructs are developing. Assessment techniques such as teachers' logs of conferences and observations and journals document change and reveal evidence of students' progress over time.

Observations and recorded notes provide critical information for the instructional team. Observation provides formative assessment to inform members of the instructional team where they need to intervene to move students forward. It can also be an evaluative tool when observing students' understandings and misunderstandings of content information reveals what they have learned.

The Guided Inquiry team can plan interventions to address specific problems and adapt strategies for guiding students throughout the inquiry. The varied expertise of the instructional team provides a way to guide students in each of the different kinds of learning, with each member observing and recording the problems and important insights in the area he or she knows best.

Reading Recovery (Clay, 1990), a successful international reading instruction program, has applied teacher observation as a valuable assessment tool. Teachers use a daily observation form on student reading to inform teaching decisions. Reading Recovery's daily observation record is a simple five-column form for teachers to record their comments and observations on different aspects of student reading. In Guided Inquiry, like Reading Recovery, observation of student learning is on each instructional team member's mind throughout the inquiry process. Members of the team are consistently observing and taking notes on what students are doing, thinking, and feeling in all five areas of inquiry learning. A five-column observation form may be provided for team members to make notes as they observe students in each of the five areas. (See Figure 8.4.) The observation form helps them to communicate their findings and design intervention to guide learning.

In Guided Inquiry observation can be extended to include what each student is engaged in; how he or she is going about the task; what comments he or she makes to another student; and how each student is using, evaluating, and synthesizing information. The librarian and teachers can go beyond attitude and general comments to include such things as an individual student's searching skill, reading comprehension, note-taking ability, reporting competence, and social interaction. These are just a very few examples of the types of learning that can be assessed through observation. These observations are based on students' performance during the inquiry unit.

Observation Form for Guided Inquiry

Date:
Students:

Students	Content	Information Literacy	Learning How to Learn	Literacy Competence	Social Skills
What students are doing					
What students are thinking					
What students are feeling					

Figure 8.4. Observation Form for Guided Inquiry.

Student Performance

The Library Power librarians also judged performance informally by noting when students show independence in applying skills, help other students, share ideas with others, ask questions, make connections, and recall at a later time. The instructional team documents how students are performing at inquiry tasks. Specifically, what are they doing to accomplish their tasks and meet their goals? Assessing students' performance requires the use of documentation of students' behavior in the inquiry process. What actions are they taking, and what thinking is prompting those actions? When documenting student performance in inquiry learning it is important to elicit the underlying thoughts that prompt students' actions. Although thoughts are difficult to uncover, there are a number of useful methods for collecting data on performance that reveal students' thinking, including journals, search logs, timelines, flowcharts, concept maps, graphic organizers, and short pieces of writing. Conferences and portfolios are two valuable methods for assessing inquiry learning. These assessment methods get inside the students' inquiry process to reveal the thinking behind their performance (Kuhlthau, 1994a).

Journals, short pieces of writing during the inquiry process, and a brief summary paragraph at the conclusion of the inquiry unit are vital interventions for Guided Inquiry (described in chapter 9). Student writings about their inquiry are also valuable methods of assessment. Journals are effective assessment tools that can track source, content, and process learning as well as providing insight into students' language and communication skills. Journals are a direct function of student performance, and through examining student journals and discussing them with the students, the instructional team can gather a good deal of assessment information about where students are and in what direction they need to go. In addition, students may be asked for short writings about their topic at several points in the inquiry process to provide a comparison for assessing change in content learning. Requiring students to write brief summary statements at the conclusion of a unit provides an evaluation of whether their content learning has gone beyond fact finding.

Charting is another valuable intervention that can be used for assessment. Concept maps, graphic organizers, timelines, and flowcharts serve as interventions as well as assessment tools. Concept maps and graphic organizers are useful for assessing content learning and ability to construct a chart of thoughts during the inquiry process. Timelines and flowcharts can depict a complex process in a one-page graphic display. Timelines can track process and flowchart can track sources.

The model of the ISP is a timeline of the inquiry process based on the thoughts, actions, and feelings that are commonly experienced by students. Students can personalize the timeline by drawing one for their own inquiry process. By drawing a line across a piece of paper and identifying the initiation of the inquiry unit at the far left and the completion of the presentation of their learning at the far right, students have a blank timeline on which to track their inquiry. The timeline represents what takes place over time, with space below the line for describing the multiple layers of experience. Students can record when they took certain steps in the inquiry process, including when they chose their topic, when they explored for their focus, when they formed a focused perspective, when they collected information, and when they presented their results. The timeline can be used to track their progress. It can be used to review what they have done after they have completed the presentation of their learning. It can also be used for planning their work at the beginning of an inquiry unit and to compare at a later time what actually took place in their inquiry process. As an assessment tool, the timeline enables the instructional team to track student performance and to assess the use of time and to guide students to plan for improvement. Younger students can complete the timeline with various levels of stickers or smiley faces to show how they are going through the process.

Flowcharts, like timelines, reveal the entire inquiry process of students related to the location and use of sources. A flowchart may be developed by placing a box in the upper lefthand corner of a sheet of paper, indicating when the inquiry began, and another box in the lower righthand corner, showing when the learning was presented. The students fill in what happened in between. The flowchart depicts an overview of the inquiry activities. This overview offers a way to assess performance, to identify problems and the need for intervention and guidance. (See Figure 8.5.)

Search logs, in which students record the sources they have located and used, may also serve as assessment tools for tracking their source learning. Students should record all the sources they locate on their inquiry topic, from the beginning of the inquiry to the close of the unit. A search log is simply a recorded list of those sources. The search log can also be used to assess the sources that students are finding and using to show the progress of the search. The search log provides a record of a student's performance in searching for information. The sources may be logged in a section of the journal, on a computer list, or in any kind of recording device, such as note cards

Conferences

The Guided Inquiry team also uses conferences to check on students' performance throughout the inquiry process, as an effective means of assessing inquiry learning. Three-member instructional teams provide more opportunities for conferencing with students. Conferences offer individualized evidence that gives an inside picture of what students are thinking, why they are taking certain actions, and how they are feeling.

Conferences help the inquiry team know how students view their own performance, where they need help, and what kinds of strategies they are using and neglecting. The knowledge gleaned from these conferences informs the intervention and helps the instructional team hone in on the specific strategies that will help students move forward.

As an example, a member of the instructional team has scheduled a short conference with each student in a grade inquiry group. The librarian meets with Lizzie. When they examine her journal together, the librarian realizes that Lizzie's note taking is a simple list of facts. Through the conversation the librarian attempts to understand if Lizzie is working to synthesize the facts. The librarian becomes aware that she needs help doing this and makes note of this so that she and the rest of the team can help Lizzie toward synthesizing. The team reports that others in the group are having similar problems. They decide to have the students organize the information from their notes in a chart to visualize the connections between their ideas. The next session with the group centers on this activity, with discussion and sharing ideas. Conferences give the instructional team opportunities for increasing students' self-awareness in their use of time, use of sources, and formulation of a focus in their inquiry.

In addition, conferences are a fundamental assessment method that separates students' ability to write from what they know. This is especially important at the younger grades, when writing is still developing. As students get older and more proficient at writing, journals can be an excellent window into their thinking. Older students' writings are a good basis for conference discussions to learn more about what they are finding difficult and what they are learning.

The team can hone in on certain aspects of student learning at conferences and record how students are interpreting the information they are finding. At other times the may team want to usher individual students through the model of the ISP to note how they are feeling and acting in the particular stage they are working through. The data gathered in these conferences lead to ways to guide instruction, intervention, and evaluation of student learning. Conferences are a major part of everyday Guided Inquiry. The collection of student work in portfolios provides a good basis for conferences with the instructional team.

Name:

Timeline Reflection on My Inquiry Process

Date	Selection	Exploration	Formulation	Collection	Completion	Assessment
Initiation	When I chose a topic	When I explored for a focus	When I formed a focus	When I collected information	When I completed the research	When I finalized the presentation
When I began the inquiry						
Thoughts						
Actions						
Feelings						

Figure 8.5. Timeline Reflection on My Inquiry Process.

Portfolios

Portfolios have been used in various ways in education. They are a useful tool when implementing a long-term, schoolwide approach that overlaps different subjects and teachers. Portfolios enable communication within an instructional team about the achievements of individual students over time. Student portfolios are an important method of assessment and evaluation in Guided inquiry

Portfolios gather evidence and artifacts that show learning across time. The Guided Inquiry team decides what will go into a portfolio during the initial planning of the inquiry unit. That planning should be sufficiently open to allow for inclusions that may not be specifically anticipated at the beginning of the project. For example, when a member of the instructional team notices that a student has made a discovery or had an "ah hah" moment, evidence may be represented in the student's portfolio. When a student has accomplished something new or used a strategy successfully, evidence can go into the portfolio. A student may realize that a piece of work shows intellectual growth and suggest that it be included. Of course, samples from final projects are good choices for inclusion in the portfolio as evidence of learning and indication of the hard work the student has put into a unit. Evidence and artifacts may come in the form of writings, notes, charts, logs, pictures, photographs, videos, and conference records. All entries should include a dated, written statement by a member of the instructional team explaining the reason and rationale for inclusion. Statements should give details about the area of learning where growth has taken place.

Portfolios are accumulated samples of students' work in progress as well as their final products. Entries need not be formal, completed pieces of student work. A variety of evidence showing the progress of learning is useful. Portfolios work well with an inquiry approach, where evidence of learning emerges naturally out of the work that students are doing. As the instructional team and students together take note of performance throughout inquiry tasks, they will choose significant documents that address progress to be placed in the portfolio.

As Guided Inquiry is a form of evidence-based practice, interventions evolve from students' need for guidance and instruction. Portfolios are substantial tools for assessing student progress in all five areas of inquiry learning. Contents of the portfolio should represent growth and learning in information literacy, inquiry process, curriculum content, reading comprehension and language development, and in some cases social interaction. Figure 8.6 shows the kinds of entries that may be included in a portfolio to show student learning in each of the five areas.

Types of Portfolio Entries for Guided Inquiry	
KINDS OF LEARNING	**EVIDENCE**
Information literacy	• Flowchart • Search log • Journal • Observation notes • Conference records • Survey results (SLIM)
Understanding learning process	• Timeline • Journal • Conference records • Survey results (SLIM)

Content area learning	• Journal • Conference records • Excerpt from final project • Short pieces of writing • Survey results (SLIM)
Literacy skills	• Conference records • Journal • Short pieces of writing • Final project • Survey results (SLIM)
Social development	• Observations notes • Journal • Self-report from student • Report from peer

Figure 8.6. Types of Portfolio Entries for Guided Inquiry.

Portfolios are a significant method for the assessment and evaluation required for Guiding Inquiry. Portfolios are also useful in showing growth and student learning to parents. Another important function of portfolios is to heighten students' awareness of their own learning and progress. The contents of a students' portfolio enable them to evaluate themselves in all five areas of inquiry learning. In this way they can become aware of where they need improvement as well as acknowledging their achievement and progress. Portfolios are excellent tools for self-reflection that leads to deep learning.

Products and Tests

One measure for evaluating student achievement is the product and presentation resulting from the inquiry unit. Evaluation of the final product provides an important piece of the entire picture. The final product is the culminating event of an inquiry unit. It represents what the student has learned. Products take many forms, such as oral presentations, festivals, demonstrations, and dramas. Products also are presented in many media, such as videos, PowerPoint™ slides, and dioramas. These products are accompanied by a written piece such as a report, paper, script, or story, with a bibliography of references.

Traditionally, it is the teacher alone who grades students' final products. In Guided Inquiry, the instructional team, the student, and the community of learners evaluate the products of inquiry. In addition to the evaluation of the instructional team, the students' evaluation of their own work provides a self-assessment for further improvement. Students also contribute to the judgment of each others' work, which opens up the evaluation to the community of learners, where each is learning from the experience of the others.

Guided Inquiry is an instructional program that stretches across the school year and extends throughout the grade levels. The instructional team gathers both evaluative and assessment information from students' final products. Through the evaluation of the final product the instructional team gathers information about what students need to accomplish in the following unit and in the next grade to further their understanding of each of the five areas of inquiry learning.

The instructional team gains a fairly good sense of what students have learned before the completion of the final product through ongoing assessment over the course of the unit. The final product, however, reveals important evidence of student learning that is not accessible until the completion of the unit. What level of synthesis has the student achieved, and how does the student present the learning? Has the student gone beyond fact finding to explain, interpret, and synthesize information and ideas? How well is the student able to communicate what he or she has learned to others?

Of course the final grade cannot be derived from the final product alone. But the final product can shed light on how students were able to accomplish their goals, how they were able to communicate what they learned to others, and how the presentation matched what they were trying to accomplish.

Tests, on the other hand, can be used to analyze how students master specific information. For example, mastery of math strategies, science formulas, and historical facts may be assessed through tests. They are often the sole tool used for grading students, but we see them as filling a particular need. A test may be the best way to find out how an entire class has learned specific facts related to the content of the unit or certain information-searching terms. However, caution should be taken not to automatically apply tests for assessing student learning. When the instructional team is considering tests, they should first determine what type of learning they are seeking to assess. Tests should be used when the information desired is best suited to a test as the evaluation instrument. Tests, combined with other assessment and evaluation methods, can provide a full picture of what has been learned in the inquiry unit.

Employing Rubrics

A rubric is a useful tool for evaluating learning. The information literacy standards include a clear definition of a rubric: "A rubric is a scaled set of criteria that clearly defines for the student and the teacher what a range of acceptable and unacceptable performances looks like. Its purpose is to provide a description of successful performances. A critical feature of rubrics is language that describes rather than labels performance. Evaluative words, like 'better,' 'more often,' and 'excellent' do not appear in rubrics. Instead, the language must precisely define actions in terms of what the student actually does to demonstrate skill or proficiency at that level" (AASL and AECT, 1998, p. 177). Rubrics are incorporated in the information literacy standards with basic, proficient, exemplary criteria of what students will be judged on in the three categories. For example, under Standard 1, "The student who is information literate accesses information efficiently and effectively," one of the indicators, "Develops and uses successful strategies for locating information," may be evaluated on three levels of proficiency: "*Basic*: Lists some ideas for how to identify and find needed information. *Proficient*: Explains and applies a plan to access needed information. *Exemplary*: Formulates and revises plans for accessing information for a range of needs and situations" (1998, p. 11).

The instructional team discusses the rubric with the students at the beginning of the inquiry unit to set the criteria for evaluation. The most effective rubrics are those in which students have an opportunity to participate in considering appropriate criteria for evaluating their work. Although the members of instructional team has thought through the rubric in advance, they are open to students' suggestions for additions and clarification. Guided Inquiry is built on careful planning by the instructional team that can adapt to students' participation as the unit progresses.

Assessing Inquiry Learning over Time

The longitudinal aspect of inquiry opens the learning process for assessment methods that provide cumulative evidence of student learning. Inquiry does not take place in one point in time, but rather involves an extended period of time of a week, month, or semester to investigate a question, topic, or problem. Longitudinal evidence reveals what takes time to develop as well as what is forgotten over time.

Longitudinal assessment provides data on students' work over time that are particularly useful for documenting change and learning. Assessment conducted at two points in time reveal what has taken place in that time period. Assessment evidence may be collected within a single unit or in a series of units over the course of a semester or school year. This provides a comparison of two or more points, with the data collected at the earlier point compared with those collected at a later point. Longitudinal assessment is used to document change in individual students' knowledge and ability and also for examining transition within a group of students.

Guided Inquiry begins in elementary school and continues on to the completion of secondary school. Assessment over several years has the potential to depict students' long-term progress. Longitudinal assessment may be used to follow students' progress over a number of school years when students have remained in the same school system. Long-term documentation of student progress requires a relatively stable population in which students are not moving in and out of the school district. Longitudinal assessment provides a way to evaluate student learning as well as assess the problems they encounter in the inquiry process.

Longitudinal assessment requires planning, organization, and management. Although students may have different teachers in each grade, librarians usually remain in place over the course of the students' progress in that school. For this reason, the librarian is uniquely positioned to provide longitudinal assessment for Guided Inquiry. The constant in Guided Inquiry teams is the school librarian, who has a continuing relationship with students from grade to grade and plays a key role in following student progress from year to year.

Self-Assessment

An important advantage of inquiry learning is that it opens opportunities for extensive self-assessment. The nature of inquiry heightens students' awareness of their experience, their ability, and their knowledge that can lead them to view themselves more objectively. When they become more reflective in assessing their progress, they are better prepared to learn from their mistakes and successes. All of the assessment methods also enable self-assessment by giving students opportunities to reflect on what they are doing as they proceed through the stages of the inquiry process.

Guided Inquiry enables students to become aware of their own navigation of the process while they are moving through the stages of inquiry. Interventions that guide students to reflect on their experience reveal their own learning process to them. Once they become aware of having experienced different stages or phases in their inquiry, they are able to plan for future situations of learning from information. Their approach to inquiry becomes more realistic, efficient, and effective. They see the purpose of developing strategies for learning within the various stages of the inquiry process, such as listing ideas and questions in the exploration stage of the ISP and taking detailed notes in the collection stage.

Interventions by the instructional team throughout the inquiry process help students to reflect on what they are feeling, doing, and thinking. However, the final stage of the inquiry process, when the presentation of learning has been completed, is a critical time for students to reflect on what they have done. At this time they can review their progress to identify what caused them difficulty and to determine what they might do differently the next time to improve. Assessment techniques such as journals, search logs, timelines, flowcharts, and short writings enable students to become more aware of their own progress through the stages of inquiry process, identify problems, and take steps toward improvement.

Developing an Instrument for Assessing Inquiry Learning: Student Surveys

The longitudinal aspect of inquiry learning offers the prospect for designing an instrument to collect data on student learning at several points in the inquiry process. An instrument for assessing inquiry learning would be a useful tool for the Guided Inquiry team. The major challenge is to design an instrument to provide assessment information for the instructional team and also promote self-awareness among students. The instrument has to be incorporated into the inquiry process without being intrusive or distracting. The ideal would be an instrument that could be used as an intervention for reflection while serving as an assessment of learning progress. To get a closer look at the assessment of inquiry learning in action, the CISSL research team conducted a study of a well-established inquiry program. The study took place at Gill St. Bernard School in Peapack, New Jersey, where inquiry learning in middle and secondary school, led by librarian Randi Schmidt, had been in place for several years. The assessment was infused into the inquiry process as a way to help students think through each stage in the process as well as give the instructional team indications of student progress.

The CISSL study at Gill St. Bernard School became a pilot study for a larger research initiative to develop an assessment instrument for inquiry learning for more general use that was funded through a research and development grant (Todd, Kuhlthau, and Heinstrom, 2005). The purpose of the project, titled "The Impact of School Libraries on Student Learning," was to develop a means for school librarians and teachers to provide evidence of the impact of their school libraries on student learning through a "toolkit" to show the growth of student learning through inquiry units. An assessment toolkit was developed, tested, and refined in the study of grades 6–12 students in ten diverse public schools in New Jersey undertaking inquiry projects. It involved teacher and school librarian teams, consisting of ten school librarians working on 17 different curriculum units with 17 classroom teachers. A full report of this research is available at www.cissl.scils.rutgers.edu/imls.

The research sought to measure how students' knowledge of their curriculum topics changed during the inquiry unit and to track changes in interest and information seeking. A combination of qualitative and quantitative methods was used to examine the students' learning. The data were collected at three stages of the students' inquiry process: at initiation of the inquiry project, midway during the inquiry process, and at the completion of the project.

Student Learning Through Inquiry Measure: SLIM

The assessment toolkit, called the Student Learning through Inquiry Measure (SLIM), was designed to

1. track changes in students' knowledge as they move through the inquiry process;

2. provide input for designing interventions for effective information seeking and learning; and

3. enable school librarians and teachers to provide evidence of the learning role of the school library.

During the development of the toolkit, student surveys were administered at three points in the inquiry process. The first survey was administered at initiation of the unit and after students had made an initial choice of a topic but before they moved to active information seeking in the exploration stage. The second survey was administered at the midpoint of the inquiry unit, after students had developed some background knowledge and were beginning to formulate a focus. The third survey was administered on the last day of the unit, after they had presented their learning. Each survey consisted of the following directions:

This short survey asks some questions about what you know about your topic and how you feel about your topic.

1. Write the title that best describes your research project at this time.

2. Take some time to think about your research topic. Now write down what you know about this topic.

3. What interests you about this topic?

4. How much do you know about this topic? Check one box that best matches how much you know.
    ☐ nothing   ☐ not much   ☐ some   ☐ quite a bit   ☐ a great deal

5. Write down what you think is easy about researching your topic.

6. Write down what you think is difficult about researching your topic.

7. Write down how you are feeling now about your project. Check only the boxes that apply to you.

    ☐ confident   ☐ disappointed   ☐ relieved   ☐ frustrated   ☐ confused
    ☐ optimistic   ☐ uncertain   ☐ satisfied   ☐ anxious   ☐ other

The third survey had three additional questions:

8. What did you learn in doing this research project? This might be about your topic or new things you can do or learn about yourself.

9. How did the school librarian help you?

10. How did the teacher help you?

When the CISSL team compared the responses on the survey at the three points in the students' inquiry process, we found that the SLIM was able to elicit change over the course of the inquiry unit. Two distinct patterns emerged in the analysis of the students' responses: fact finding and synthesis. One pattern focused on fact finding and the other focused on interpreting to determine what the facts mean.

In the fact-finding pattern students accumulated over the course of the three surveys. These students listed general "commonsense" facts in the first survey, an increased number of facts in the second survey, and more facts in the third survey. An example of a fact-finding pattern is shown in the students' statements taken from the three surveys. Survey 1, "He is very famous for his plays . . . "; Survey 2, "He married Anne Hathaway. They had 3 children. He wrote 37 plays and 152 sonnets."; Survey 3, "He was born on April 23, 1564 in Stratford-upon-Avon, Britain . . . . Married at age 18. Had three children, Judith, Hammet and Sussana. He was the first boy in the family, had 3 sisters and 1 brother, Joan, Margaret, Gilbert." Statements on the second and third surveys add more facts, but there was little relationship or connection between the facts made over the course of the inquiry unit.

In the comparison of the three surveys, the synthesis pattern showed a change in students' use of facts. The students listed general "commonsense" facts in the first survey similar to the fact-finding students. However, in the second survey these students' statements showed explanation of how and why and/or an indication of making connections and linking the facts. In the third survey many of these students' statements showed evidence of interpreting the facts and drawing conclusions. The statements of these students on the third survey were sometimes shorter and more concise than their second survey statements.

An example of a synthesis pattern is shown in one student's statements taken from the three surveys. The student's topic was the immune system. Survey 1, "It probably has most to do with how the body reacts to certain problems in the body. Like how a body reacts to a sneeze or a cough."; Survey 2, "The immune system is what protects you, anybody from various outside bacteria, viruses, and germs. The immune has I-cells and other types of cells that help fight the . . . . When you cut yourself you can see the immune system at work because you can see the cells that are rebuilding the tissues that were cut . . . etc."; Survey 3, "The immune system was a big topic. I found out that there is actually two types of immune systems in the body . . . . I learned that if bacteria enters your body, it could enter a cell, replicate in a matter of minutes . . . . So you have millions of bacteria in the body after an hour . . . . The body works against such organ [degradation], mineral deficiency, mechanical damage and other. What I really enjoyed to learn was that the minute you are born . . . and when you die your immune system shuts down letting in all the bad stuff, so now the body is an open door."

Another example of a synthesis pattern was taken from the statements of a student investigating the topic of adrenalin. Survey 1, "It is a natural rush in your body. It can occur from excitement, nervousness or fear. Can enable a mother to lift a car off her child: a strong rush of energy strength or feeling."; Survey 2, "It is a compound that is stimulated by a feeling of fear, excitement or nervousness. It effects nerve and muscle functions and effects circulatory system and heart rate. It can be used in asthma inhalers to relax outbursts and attacks. Also called epinephrine."; Survey 3, "Adrenaline or epinephrine is a hormone. It forms clear to white crystals and is effected by light and dark. It is created in the medulla . . . from the hypothalamus part of the brain. It is known as the 'fight or flight' response that prepares your body for a big mental or physical act. It effects normal muscle use, lungs . . . . It is used in asthma inhalers, operations to prevent bleeding and used in cardiac arrest injections."

These two examples of synthesis show quite sophisticated, progressive use of information for learning that had been acquired by these students over the course of project and clearly point to what can be done in Guided Inquiry. The fact-finding example shows an opportunity for intervention that guides students to reflect on the facts they are finding and to begin to look for explanations and conclusions.

The third survey question is related to students' interest over the course of the unit. Students in schools with the most explanation and conclusions in their responses showed stronger positive emotions at the projects' completion when compared with students with more of a fact-finding pattern. In response to questions about what was easy and difficult, students' statements related to the availability and access of information. Responses to how librarians and teachers helped described the traditional role of the teacher helping with content and the librarian helping with sources.

There was a substantial difference in student learning in different projects, but the teachers and librarians were not fully aware of the differences. This may have been because they didn't have effective instruments to assess student learning. Some inquiry units resulted in more fact finding and others resulted in more explanation and interpretation of the facts. Surprisingly, these patterns were not found to be related to the age or ability of the students. It seemed to be related to what the students expected to do in the inquiry unit and the interventions that guided them through their inquiry. This finding was similar to the Limberg study (1997), in which the objective of the students determined how they approached the inquiry project, whether they thought it was a fact-finding exercise or understood that they needed to reflect on the facts and come up with some ideas of their own about the topic of inquiry. When we reported these findings to the expert librarians in the study, they began to think of strategies for guiding their students in going beyond fact finding to drawing conclusions for deeper learning. This is the very purpose of an assessment tool. However, the drawback of the SLIM at this point was that the librarians and teachers didn't have criteria to use to evaluate the students' statements. The CISSL research team had developed a system of coding the surveys that could not easily be reproduced for teachers and librarians to apply in their schools.

Although SLIM was successful for eliciting change in students' knowledge over the course of an inquiry unit, it was difficult to analyze. The study provided insight into the development of an assessment instrument for inquiry learning and raised some considerations for adapting the SLIM for broad use. Some of the teachers and librarians in the study reported that the surveys took too much time. A shortened version of SLIM included five similar questions, with a sixth on the third survey. The surveys were called "reflection tasks" to encourage their use as interventions to help students reflect on what they were doing and to foster self-assessment as well as serving as an assessment tool for the instructional team:

Reflection task 1

1. Take some time to think about your topic. Now write down what you know about it.

2. How interested are you in this topic? Check one box that best matches your interest.

    ☐ not at all   ☐ not much   ☐ quite a bit   ☐ a great deal

3. How much do you know about this topic? Check one box that best matches how much you know.

    ☐ not at all   ☐ not much   ☐ quite a bit   ☐ a great deal

4. When you do research, what do you find easy to do?

5. When you do research, what do you find difficult to do?

Reflection task 2

4. Thinking of your research so far, what did you find easy to do?

5. Thinking of your research so far, what did you find difficult to do?

Reflection task 3

4. Thinking back on your research project, what did you find easy to do?

5. Thinking back on your research project, what did you find most difficult to do?

6. What did you learn in doing this research project?

The CISSL team devised a procedure for analyzing and comparing the students' statements on the three reflection tasks, intended for use by instructional teams of teachers and librarians (see Figure 8.7). The coding identifies facts, explanations, and conclusions in student statements to questions 1, 2, and 6, which relate to curriculum content learning. Most responses to questions 4 and 5, regarding what is easy and difficult, related to information location, evaluation, and use and may be assessed on an individual basis to determine where the student needs assistance, guidance, and instruction during the inquiry process.

Analyzing SLIM Reflection Tasks	
Area of Learning Assessed	**Questions**

Curricular content
  Facts
  Explanations
  Conclusions
	1. Take some time to think about your topic. Now write down what you know about it.
	2. How interested are you in this topic?
	6. What did you learn in doing this research project?

Process of learning over time	3. How much do you know about this topic?

Information literacy
  Location
  Evaluation
  Use
	4. When you do research, what do you find easy to do?
	5. Thinking of your research so far, what did you find difficult to do?

Figure 8.7. Analyzing SLIM Reflection Tasks.

Preliminary testing found that some teams found it a useful tool for collecting data and coding and analyzing the students' responses. Those who found it useful commented that it helped them check whether students were learning throughout the project. The SLIM toolkit is available on the CISSL Web site at www.cissl.scils.rutgers.edu/.

Many Ways of Assessing for Guided Inquiry

In this chapter we discussed the importance of both evaluation and assessment in Guided Inquiry. Assessment is essential for guiding students through the process of learning from a variety of sources. However, assessment is complicated because there are different kinds of learning going on at the same time. Students are learning about sources, content, process, comprehension and articulation abilities, and social skills. No one measure can capture it all. The SLIM toolkit has been found to be useful for assessing many of these kinds of learning. However, SLIM is only one way of assessing learning. The most effective assessment combines several measures such as SLIM with observation portfolios and conferences to give a fuller picture of students' progress and need for further intervention. By taking advantage of the longitudinal aspect of inquiry learning, assessment may be done at different points in the process to provide a comparison for demonstrating change or monitoring the need for intervention.

The most successful assessment techniques are those that can be folded into the inquiry process. Students and teachers become impatient with assessment that interrupts the process of learning and distracts students from the task at hand. By incorporating assessment measures with intervention strategies, the dual purpose of helping students to reflect on their work in progress and providing an assessment of their work for the instructional team is accomplished. Many intervention strategies that promote reflection intended to foster comprehension also provide data for assessment These interventions also provide the necessary feedback for student self-assessment, essential for learning.

In a follow-up survey of teams of teachers and librarians who had participated in Guided Inquiry workshops, many noted an improvement in their students' learning. While they recognized that an inquiry approach took more time than previous years' projects, they also noted that the learning was richer and deeper and that "knowledge became more personalized over time." As they saw improvement in their students' learning, they noted that the inquiry approach was beginning to take hold in their schools. As one team reported, "The project was initially intended as one project but gave birth to new projects along the way that all were connected." Once they had adopted the Guided Inquiry approach with their students, they continued in other projects as new questions and topics arose along the way. Connections in the pursuit of learning are an integral part of the inquiry process that teaches students the natural progression of constructing their understandings of their world.

This chapter discussed assessment as an essential component of Guided Inquiry, presenting research that shows the impact of school libraries on learning in a series of studies of students', librarians', and teachers' assessment of learning. Observation, performance, products, and tests identified as indicators of learning are being developed into strategies to assess student learning through the inquiry process. Journals, search logs, timelines, flowcharts, conferences, and portfolios are among the assessment strategies recommended along with suggestions for employing rubrics. SLIM, Student Learning through Inquiry Measure, designed specifically for Guided Inquiry, was introduced. The best assessment is embedded in the inquiry process and folded into the interventions guiding the inquiry.

Interventions for Guiding Inquiry

Intervention is what we used to call the teachable moment—the moment when somebody can learn more about the research process or about the content or where to find something.
—middle school librarian

Guided Inquiry is based on intervention at critical points in students' progress through the inquiry process. The instructional team organizes the unit of study and identifies critical points at which students need assistance and instruction to progress in their learning. When to intervene and how to intervene in students' inquiry are the main decisions for the Guided Inquiry team in planning a unit. This chapter examines the theoretical concept underlying decisions about when to intervene. Fundamental considerations and practical ideas are discussed.

Guided Inquiry is a perspective on learning rather than a formula for teaching. The very nature of inquiry makes it impractical to present a prescribed package for implementing inquiry learning in all schools for every student. The definition of Guided Inquiry discussed in the first chapter is worth repeating at this point to keep in mind the dynamic, evolving nature of inquiry learning and the flexibility and professional expertise called for in the instructional team.

Inquiry is an approach to learning that involves students in finding and using a variety of sources of information and ideas to increase their understanding of a specific area of the curriculum. It is not simply answering questions and getting the right answers. Inquiry learning engages, interests, and challenges students to connect their world with the curriculum. Inquiry does not stand alone but is grounded in the content of the curriculum, which motivates students to question, explore, and formulate new ideas. Although it is often thought of as an individual pursuit, inquiry is enhanced by involvement with a community of learners in social interaction where each can learn from the other. Inquiry is a way of learning that prepares students to think for themselves, make thoughtful decisions, develop areas of expertise, and learn throughout their lives. It is a way of learning that meets the demands of living in the information-driven society of the 21st century. Students gain competence in inquiry learning by being guided through the inquiry process by teams of teachers and librarians at each grade level. We call this guided approach to inquiry learning Guided Inquiry.

In this chapter we examine some general principles and strategies for guiding students in the development of knowledge and skills for learning from a variety of sources of information. Although each Guided Inquiry unit should be tailored to specific students meeting certain curriculum standards, there are some general guidelines for developing interventions that the instructional team should consider when planning for students. Interventions are carefully planned by the Guided Inquiry team with the objective of enabling students to develop research competency and subject knowledge as well as fostering cooperative learning, reading comprehension, language development, and social skills.

In Guided Inquiry we use the term "intervention" instead of "instruction." Instruction is only one type of intervention used by the team. Many others are discussed in this chapter. This difference in terminology orients our thinking about guiding student inquiry, which is at the core of designing and implementing inquiry learning for students.

Open-Ended Questions

First and foremost, Guided Inquiry is initiated by treating issues, questions, and problems as open-ended ones that must be addressed by using a number of sources over a period of time. These open-ended topics arise directly from the subject areas of the curriculum to initiate inquiry based in research rather than artificially imposed research assignments that only peripherally relate to the context, content, and objectives of the course of study. Open-ended topics provide opportunities for students to generate questions that are important and interesting to them. Through modeling, conversing, and listening, the instructional team guides students in raising their own questions, which motivate them to investigate to learn more. Research on student engagement and motivation has found that self-generated topics are pursued more deeply and with greater interest than those that students perceive as imposed on them (Gross, 1998; McNally, 2005). The Guided Inquiry team issues an invitation to research that draws students into the inquiry process.

The open-ended questions of Guided Inquiry can be compared to the essential questions of *Understanding by Design* (Wiggins and McTighe, 1998). In the backward design process of *Understanding by Design*, teachers are encouraged to "first identify the desired learning outcome" and work backward to "determine what is acceptable evidence" before "planning learning experiences and instruction" (p. 9). In Guided Inquiry, the core team plans carefully and considers at the beginning of the inquiry what outcomes will be the result as well as what assessments will be used to determine learning and understanding. In addition, the core team plans assessments and interventions throughout the process of the inquiry that are directed or targeted to each student's competences and needs.

In Guided Inquiry students are encouraged to "address" questions rather than "answer" them. Looking for answers promotes fact finding for the right answer. While finding a right answer to a simple question may be incorporated into the inquiry process from time to time, the purpose of inquiry is learning at a higher level. Looking for answers promotes a simplistic approach that stops at fact finding, neglecting reflection on what the facts mean. Inquiry is based on investigation for deeper understanding. Guided Inquiry involves students in addressing open-ended questions for constructing their own deep understanding of a specific area of the curriculum. Addressing questions leads students into interesting directions to explore ideas and arrive at new understandings.

The Guided Inquiry team designs inquiry assignments that create an invitational tone or mood to initiate the inquiry process. An assignment can set either an invitational mood or an indicative mood at the beginning, which influences students' attitudes and approach throughout the entire inquiry process (Kuhlthau, 2004). Assignments that set an indicative mood are prescriptive, narrow, and simplistic and tend to close down the inquiry before it begins. An assignment that sets an invitational mood opens up the creative possibilities that inquiry allows. Guided Inquiry teams seek to design inquiry assignments that foster an invitational mood through open-ended questions for students to address through the inquiry process.

Basic Inquiry Abilities

There are basic abilities that underlie the inquiry process. These abilities can be introduced to the youngest child in prekindergarten and developed throughout elementary school. These abilities can be applied to extensive inquiry projects in middle school and expanded to more independent projects in secondary school.

- Recall—Remember what stands out in your mind.
- Summarize—Select ideas and place them in meaningful sequence.
- Paraphrase—Tell it in your own words.
- Extend—Form new understandings and raise new questions.

Memory plays a critical function in the process of learning. In the Guided inquiry context, recalling is reflecting and remembering certain features of what has been read, heard, and observed. We remember selectively rather than recalling everything. *Recall* is based on what we already know, which forms a frame of reference for selective remembering. The personal frame of reference is often referred to as a person's schema or constructs. What is recalled is a selective process that may differ widely from child to child. Recalling personal experiences that relate to the ideas encountered through the inquiry process helps children select those that have personal meaning. Guided Inquiry encourages students to recall, enabling them to make connections with what they already know and to note what fits or contradicts their present constructs. Children might ask each other, "What surprised you?" or "What did you find interesting?" Recall is not merely reciting back but active remembering on the part of the student.

Summarizing is organizing selected ideas in a meaningful sequence. Like recalling, summarizing involves selective attention that is based on the child's former constructs. Constructs lead children to consider certain ideas significant and others less so. Intervention that encourages students to summarize enables them to select salient points, facts, and themes from information and to order the ideas in a meaningful way: not what the textbook prescribes as important points, but what the student sees as important. Looking at the text in this way and knowing that this is what we want students to do is an important attribute of inquiry learning. This type of personal summarizing must be modeled, taught, valued, and emphasized over and over. What is left out is as important a choice as what is retained.

The decision about what is enough to convey meaning is the difficult conceptual task of formulation. Small children tend to want to tell all and have difficulty choosing parts of a story. For older children the author's words sound better than their own. Without clear value of students' own summaries, mindless transport of texts or copying will usually result. The main objective of summarizing is to organize the information in an abbreviated form by determining the ideas that convey personal meaning. Guided Inquiry enables students to summarize, preparing them to use information to formulate and build their own ideas in the process of learning through inquiry. Children might ask each other, "What do you think is important?" "What comes at the beginning, in the middle, at the end?"

Paraphrasing is retelling in one's own words the ideas encountered in the inquiry process. When children's words are as acceptable as the author's and more appropriate under certain circumstances, they are encouraged to break away from the text to tell the story in their own way. When we talk about texts, we are talking about all sort of multimedia, such as interviews, films, and art, as well as books and other printed materials. Through Guided Inquiry young children's retelling and paraphrasing is valued and encouraged. Where paraphrasing is not valued, indiscriminate copying and plagiarism frequently results. Inquiry arises from an open-ended question to be addressed, a problem to be solved, or an issue to be explored that requires paraphrasing ideas. It is not a simple question to be answered by copying word for word from a text. However, it is essential that the origin of the information be documented and the author credited. Guided Inquiry helps students to determine when to use their own words and what to quote and how to document their sources. Paraphrasing is a powerful ability for formulating and learning in the inquiry process. Children might ask each other to, "Tell about what you learned" or "Tell what was interesting and new."

Extending is forming new understandings and raising new questions. Extending involves making connections between ideas gathered through the inquiry process and one's own constructs. In literacy and reading comprehension, students are encouraged to make connections between the source and themselves, other texts, and the world. Extending begins with a thorough and explicit comprehension of the source, leading to the interpretation of the ideas within. It encompasses interpreting information and applying it in the creative process of using information. Extending is an essential ability in learning that leads students beyond mere fact finding and question answering to explanation, synthesis, and creating a deep understanding of their own. Children might ask each other "What connects with something else you know?" "How does it relate to something you have read, seen, or done?" "What else would you like to know?" Guided Inquiry challenges students to seek meaning in the inquiry process and to apply their learning to their own lives. "What if" questions are also good for eliciting deep thinking in extending to form new understandings. (see Figure 9.1.)

Intervention Questions for Basic Inquiry Abilities	
Recall	Remember what stands out in your mind. • What surprised you? • What did you find interesting?
Summarize	Select ideas and place them in a meaningful sequence. • What do you think is important? • What comes at the beginning, middle, and end?
Paraphrase	Tell it in your own words. • What was interesting and new? • Tell about what you learned.
Extend	Form new understandings and raise new questions. • How does it relate to something else you have read, seen, or done? • What else would you like to know?

Figure 9.1. Intervention Questions for Basic Inquiry Abilities.

Guided Inquiry develops students' ability to recall, summarize, paraphrase, and extend information and ideas, enabling them to learn through inquiry. These four abilities are interwoven with all stages of the inquiry process rather than occurring in a step-by-step sequence. As students encounter ideas, new questions arise that require further information. This recursive process leads to formulation of a focused perspective and a depth of understanding. In this program of Guided Inquiry, these abilities are introduced and developed in grades prekindergarten–2, reinforced in grades 3–5, and applied in the middle and secondary school with multiple sources from a variety of formats. Developing these basic inquiry abilities in the early grades lays the foundation for learning through the inquiry process in middle school and independent inquiry in secondary school, which paves the way for lifelong learning in the information age.

Strategies for Inquiry Learning

In Guided Inquiry the instructional team employs intervention strategies for enabling students to construct their own understandings. These strategies are recommended for helping students to move beyond fact finding to explanation and synthesis of the facts. Chapter 3 discusses how collaboration and conversation are applied for creating third space, where the curriculum and the child's world merge, and for forming a community of learners. This section includes four additional strategies and discusses some ways each may be applied in Guided Inquiry. These intervention strategies, known as the "Six Cs", are collaborate, converse, continue, choose, chart, and compose (Kuhlthau, 2004, pp. 134–140). (See Figure 9.2.)

Intervention Strategies for Guided Inquiry	
The Six Cs	
1. Collaborate	Work jointly with others.
2. Converse	Talk about ideas for clarity and further questions.
3. Continue	Develop understanding over a period of time.
4. Choose	Select what is interesting and pertinent.
5. Chart	Visualize ideas using pictures, timelines, and graphic organizers.
6. Compose	Write all the way along, not just at end; keep journals.

Figure 9.2. Intervention Strategies for Guided Inquiry.

Collaboration enables students to try out ideas, raise questions, and hear other perspectives at various stages in the inquiry process. As we have discussed, inquiry is not an isolated, competitive undertaking in Guided Inquiry but rather a cooperative venture in a community of learners. Students often find that consulting with classmates enables them to clarify their ideas and to learn from each other. In Guided Inquiry students benefit from collaborating even though they are involved in different topics or different aspects of the same topic. Carefully organized, flexible, small groups and work pairs in which students are not always in the same groupings enable them to take full advantage of working in a community of learners. Collaboration diminishes the experience of isolation in inquiry and enables students to help each other in the process of learning. Collaborative strategies such as brainstorming, delegating, networking, and integrating are productive activities for learning through inquiry as well as developing abilities valued in the world outside school.

Conversation enables students to articulate their thoughts, identify gaps, and clarify inconsistencies in the inquiry process. Conversing helps students to think through the ideas they are encountering. The instructional team gives structure to the conversations by providing discussion starters such as, "What ideas seem important, interesting, or surprising? What fits in with your thinking and what doesn't fit?" Conversation as an intervention strategy also helps students work through the stages of the inquiry process. Conversation at the early stages opens up the possibilities for inquiry. During the exploration stage, conversation enables students to share their feelings of confusion and uncertainty and to receive support and suggestions on how to proceed. After focus formulation, conversation centers on explaining the meaning of the information and facts students are collecting. Conversation also helps students to identify ways to organize their ideas for presenting what they have learned. The instructional team guides the conversation, allowing students to express their thoughts and feelings through listening and modeling, then stepping in at critical points, the zones of intervention.

Continuing promotes students' awareness that inquiry involves active engagement over time. Continuing strategies support students throughout the inquiry process. Intervention continues in each stage of the process to guide students in their use of information for learning and constructing from the ideas encountered in a variety of sources. Continuing strategies help students to understand that constructing a personal understanding is a process that requires time. When they become aware of the stages in their inquiry process they begin to see that inquiry involves more than selecting a topic, collecting facts, and reporting. Learning through inquiry involves not only gathering information but also reading, reflecting, raising questions, and exploring ideas over an extended period of time to construct new understandings. Intervention is designed to help students think about where they are in the inquiry process and to offer advice on proceeding with the particular task they are confronting. Guided Inquiry supports students with advice and guidance that continues throughout the inquiry process.

Choosing enables students to learn how to take control of their own information-seeking process. In Guided Inquiry the instructional team develops interventions that help students learn that inquiry requires making choices: choosing a topic, choosing sources, choosing ideas in the sources, choosing what to pursue, choosing what to leave out, choosing what is enough. These interventions help students base their choices on the criteria of time, task, interest, and availability. How much time do I have? What am I trying to accomplish? What am I interested in? What information is available? Some choices are more important than others for shaping the direction of the inquiry and the formulation of the topic. Choices that lead to forming a focus establish the direction and extent of the inquiry. Once a focus or guiding idea has been formed, students have a frame of reference for choosing what is useful and what is not useful in the sources they are gathering. The instructional team provides interventions that enable students to learn how to select what is interesting and pertinent based on the information literacy concepts presented in chapter 6. Good choices are those that lead students to create their own understandings rather than thoughtlessly copying and reproducing text. Through intervention students learn that what they choose may not be the same as what another student chooses. Guided Inquiry enables students to become aware that choosing is a creative strategy that allows them to select what they find interesting and want to pursue in the inquiry process.

Charting enables students to present a large amount of information in a compact way. It is a useful strategy for all five types of intervention: curriculum content; information literacy; learning how to learn; reading, writing, and speaking competencies; and social skills. When students become aware that each of these aspects of inquiry can be visualized in a chart, they begin to understand the complexity of what they are experiencing. Charting applies visualization as another way of knowing that enhances the learning process. Concept maps and graphic organizers are excellent tools for connecting ideas and organizing information. Timelines, flowcharts, and drawings are useful for visualizing the inquiry process, the sources located and used, and the ideas that are emerging. Interventions that employ charting help students to visualize ideas, issues, questions, and strategies that emerge during the inquiry process. Charting enables students to visualize the entire inquiry process from initiation to presentation and to anticipate what to expect in each stage. By displaying and discussing the chart of the model of the ISP, shown in Figure 2.2 (p. 18), the team can help them can identify what stage of the inquiry process they are in and offer instruction and advice for accomplishing the task of each stage, using Figure 8.5 (p. 121).

Composing promotes thinking throughout the inquiry process. Journal writing is a well-established strategy for reflection and construction that may be applied throughout the process. Students keep inquiry journals to record facts, ideas, questions, and connections as they progress through their inquiry. They need to set aside time each day to write in their journals. Writing in an inquiry journal is more comprehensive than jotting notes on cards or in a notebook. The inquiry journals are started when the project is first initiated, with students recording their early thoughts and feelings. The purpose of the inquiry journals changes as the inquiry progresses. They become idea and source logs as the students work through the exploration stage and a detailed notebook in the later stages after they have formed a focus, with connections and plans for presenting their learning as the inquiry comes to a close. The main objective of an inquiry journal is to serve as a tool for formulating thoughts and developing constructs over the course of the inquiry unit.

Composing enables the construction of new ideas and learning. It is also a useful tool for tracking progress and identifying the need for an individual conference to guide a particular student. Another effective intervention using composing is having the students write short pieces about their topic at three points in the inquiry process, at the beginning, middle, and end. These short pieces of writing help students to see what they have formulated and what is missing as well as to alert the instructional team about individual students requiring assistance. This strategy is also applied for assessing learning (discussed in chapter 8). In many inquiry units, composing is the way the learning is presented by each of the students at end of the inquiry process. In Guided Inquiry the audience for the final written product is the community of learners, comprising the other students as well as the instructional team.

Zones of Intervention

The zone of intervention is a concept modeled on Vygotsky, the Soviet psychologist, whose work had a profound influence on learning theory. Vygotsky (1978) developed the concept of identifying an area or zone in which intervention would be most helpful to a learner. The zone of proximal development is the distance between the actual developmental level of the learner as determined by independent problem solving and the level of potential development as determined through problem solving under professional guidance or in collaboration with more capable peers (p. 131). This concept provides a model for understanding intervention in the inquiry process of students.

Similarly, the zone of intervention in the inquiry process may be thought of as where the teacher helps the student to a higher level of thinking. The zone of intervention is "that area in which the student can do with advice and assistance what he or she cannot do alone or can do only with great difficulty" (Kuhlthau, 2004, pp. 128–129). Intervention within this zone enables students to progress in the accomplishment of their task. Intervention outside this zone is inefficient and unnecessary, experienced by students as intrusive on the one hand and overwhelming on the other. In addition, intervention outside this zone does not make efficient use of the valuable time and talent of the Guided Inquiry team.

The ISP model describes the experience and behavior of students involved in extensive research projects. Students often have difficulty in the early phases of the inquiry process. Even when they begin with enthusiasm and initial success, many soon become confused and uncertain how to proceed. Rather than experiencing a steady increase in confidence from the beginning of an inquiry project to the conclusion, they commonly have a dip in confidence once they have initiated the inquiry and begin to encounter conflicting and inconsistent information. A person "in the dip" is increasingly uncertain and confused until a focus is formed to provide a path for seeking meaning and criteria for judging relevance.

The dip in confidence seems to be a natural stage in the process of constructing new knowledge. When the inquiry process is viewed as a process of construction, the work of Kelly, Dewey, and Bruner explaining similar situations in which students are actively engaged in learning becomes a useful framework for understanding the inquiry process. Each of these theorists described the constructive process as occurring in a sequence of stages or phases, to be actively worked through by the individual. Uncertainty common in the earlier stages increases with the introduction of new information that conflicts with previously held constructs.

Advances in information technology that open access to a vast assortment of sources have not helped the student's dilemma of uncertainty and in many cases have intensified the sense of confusion and uncertainty. Information search systems may deepen the problem, particularly at the beginning, by overwhelming the student with everything all at once when a few well-chosen pieces might be more useful for constructive learning. This is why in Guided Inquiry a large part of the instructional team's work is assisting students through those troubling times of uncertainty.

The model of the ISP from Kuhlthau's research clearly reveals that students holistically experience the inquiry process with their thoughts and actions interacting with their feelings. Students' feelings have as great an impact on how they pursue their inquiry as their thoughts and their actions. Negative feelings are one indication that intervention is needed to enable students to move along in their inquiry. We have noted that certain times in the inquiry process are particularly troubling and confusing for students.

One way that the instructional team is clued into when students need intervention is through noticing their reactions and feelings during the ISP. When students are uncertain or confused, we can take that as a cue to step in with a specific intervention. Kuhlthau's studies were among the first to investigate the affective aspects or the feelings of a person in the process of information seeking along with the cognitive and physical aspects. One of the important findings was the discovery of a sharp increase in uncertainty and decrease in confidence after a search had been initiated during the exploration stage. Students tend to think that they are the only ones to experience increased uncertainty and are relieved to find that this is a common occurrence. Increased uncertainty indicates a need for intervention in the inquiry process. The concept of a zone of intervention offers the Guided Inquiry team a way to make decisions regarding interventions that are enabling and enriching for their students and enables the instructional team to analyze students' tasks and to tailor intervention to specific ones.

Intervention for Five Kinds of Learning

Guided inquiry is composed of an inquiry unit that engages students in their own learning, with instruction and guidance at strategic points along the way, in the zone of intervention. Learning through inquiry involves a number of different things going on at the same time, each requiring a different type of intervention. Students are looking for sources of information and need advice on how to find useful, relevant, and pertinent sources of facts and ideas for their project. They need intervention to develop *information literacy*. At the same time, they are experiencing the process of learning from the information in these sources, described in the model of the ISP. They need intervention to develop *learning strategies*. They are also learning content from the sources that may cause confusion about subject concepts. They require intervention to learn *curriculum content*. They also may be having difficulty comprehending what they are reading or articulating what they are thinking. They need intervention for improving *literacy competency*. In addition, when they are working in groups they need intervention for developing *social skills*.

Each kind of learning requires interventions targeted to that learning (see Figure 9.3). For example, each intervention fosters and develops specific skills and processes. Intervention to foster learning curriculum content involves building knowledge of subject content through fact finding, interpreting, and synthesizing information in sources located during the inquiry process. Information literacy intervention develops competence in locating, evaluating, and using information and understanding information literacy concepts. Learning strategies intervention develops ability for learning how to learn and involves understanding one's own learning process through awareness of the stages of the ISP. Literacy intervention improves reading comprehension, language development, and writing ability. Social skills intervention develops ability to interact with others in situations that require cooperating and collaborating.

Interventions for Learning in the Inquiry Process	
Five Kinds of Learning	**Types of Intervention**
Curriculum Content	for fact finding, interpreting, and synthesizing
Information Literacy	for locating, evaluating, and using information
Learning How to Learn	for initiating, selecting, exploring, focusing, collecting, and presenting
Literacy Competence	for improving reading, writing, speaking, and listening
Social Skills	for interacting, cooperating, and collaborating

Figure 9.3. Interventions for Learning in the Inquiry Process.

It takes considerable expertise and attention on the part of the instructional team to guide students in each of these at the time they most need help. Students will need different types of intervention in Guided Inquiry: curriculum content, information literacy, learning how to learn, literacy competency, and social skills. It is important to remember that the instructional team is built around expertise in each of these types of intervention. The school librarian has expertise in information literacy intervention, and teachers in curriculum content intervention. The whole team brings their combined expertise for intervention that promotes learning how to learn and for developing social skills. Some students may need assistance in reading or writing beyond what the subject area teacher and librarian can provide. In this case a learning skills or literacy specialist may join the team to provide learning skills intervention.

Information literacy intervention develops students' knowledge and skills for locating, evaluating, and using information from a variety of resources. At the beginning of an inquiry unit it may be helpful to present an overview of recommended information sources to orient students to the range of materials available for their inquiry. However, detailed instruction on locating and using particular sources will be most effective at the time when the materials will be used. This zone of intervention is what librarians call "point of use" instruction. Interventions that incorporate the information literacy concepts, presented and discussed in chapter 5, enable students to develop deep understanding of principles and strategies for locating and using a variety of sources of information. In the instructional team, the school librarian takes the lead on information literacy intervention.

Curriculum content intervention provides students with knowledge of the subjects that are defined in the objectives of the inquiry unit that have been selected from the curriculum standards. Numerous subject area curriculum standards in math, science, language arts, and social studies may be met through Guided Inquiry, as discussed in chapter 6. There are also numerous opportunities for interdisciplinary inquiry, which draws on two subject areas for enhancing the content of each. The zone of intervention for enabling students to understand content is sometimes known as the "teachable moment" or "critical learning point" (William and Wavell, 2006, p. 17). A variety of interventions guide students to go beyond fact finding to reflect on the meaning of the facts for their own deep understanding of content. In the instructional team, subject teachers take the lead on content intervention.

Through Guided Inquiry students learn subject area content while also developing research competence in that subject discipline. Each discipline has research methods and special sources that are specific to that subject area. Subject teachers understand how research is conducted in their field of specialization and can plan tactics with the librarian that match subject area inquiry. For example, research on an event in history, literary criticism, and science investigation all call for different methods of inquiry and different sources of information. By the time students are in secondary school, they can tailor their information seeking to the subject under study.

Interventions for learning how to learn develop students' understanding of the stages of the inquiry process and a sense of their own learning in the process. As we have discussed, one of the most critical zones of intervention in the inquiry process is the exploration stage. In exploration, after students have selected a general area to pursue within the main topic, but before they have formulated their own ideas from the information, they are gathering into a focus or guiding idea. Intervention in this time of confusion helps students learn how to construct their own knowledge from a variety of sources of information.

Students gain a sense of control of their own learning process by understanding what to expect while investigating different, often conflicting, sources of information and ideas. Learning process intervention introduces strategies for working through the difficult stages of learning. The instructional team joins together to provide intervention that develops learning how to learn throughout the inquiry process.

Literacy intervention enables students to comprehend the materials they find and to articulate what they have learned. The reading teacher, in the case study presented in chapter 4, played this role in the instructional team. She worked with individual students who needed assistance in reading the material they found, taking notes on important ideas, and preparing to present what they had learned. This intervention enabled these students to successfully engage in the inquiry process. At the same time, these students were improving their reading comprehension in a practical, applied way. In the case study, the principal was particularly impressed to see that students at all levels were able to engage in inquiry and to learn from each other. The reading teacher or literacy specialist makes a substantial contribution to the instructional team when students can benefit from this type of intervention.

Guided Inquiry lends itself to differentiated learning. Differentiated classrooms (Tomlinson, 1999) are those that allow for students of different abilities to work together. Guided Inquiry is a prime example, with flexible grouping and targeted interventions aimed at specific needs. Targeted literacy intervention gives students opportunities to move from learning to read, to reading to learn, and applying that learning in a meaningful way.

The instructional team will need to plan for all of these kinds of intervention and determine the optimal zone of intervention to provide the most productive learning for their students. The team will need considerable flexibility to make the most of the flow of ideas and problems that arise as students' inquiry progresses. One way to accomplish this is by being alert to students' interests and needs that arise from their world both inside and outside school.

Connecting to the Students' World

Guided Inquiry is grounded in the constructivist perspective that clearly recognizes the necessity of connecting to a student's own world in meeting curriculum standards. In chapter 3 we discuss the importance of creating third space, where the students' personal experiences interact with the content of the curriculum. The students' world and the curriculum are two separate, unconnected spaces. Students left on their own to make the connections often find little relationship between the two. The Guided Inquiry team plans interventions that enable third space interaction, in which the students' experiences and the curriculum merge to provide a dynamic, meaningful learning environment. Third space interaction promotes motivation and interest throughout the inquiry process and lasting learning after the project is completed. The master teacher in the case study in chapter 3 applied conversing, modeling, and listening as interventions for creating third space with her students. Conversing is the overall intervention used in this case study, where students were organized in small groups to talk about books they were reading. Modeling gives students an example to follow for sharing their experiences in conversation with others. Listening is used as an intervention to pay close attention to what students are saying and to respond in ways that encourage and respect their contributions. The teachers' listening is also a model for students to follow in conversation with each other. Analysis of these conversations shows the complexity of interaction and depth of learning in third space that these interventions fostered. They are good examples for adopting conversation as an intervention for connecting to the students' world in Guided Inquiry.

The extended KWL questions for Guided Inquiry, discussed in chapter 1, offer another way to think about designing interventions that connect to the students' world. These six questions provide a brief outline of the kind of interventions that seek to draw on students' personal experiences. "What do I know?" is intended to call on students' prior knowledge and lead to first space revelations. However, students' responses to this question may merely parrot what the students think the teacher wants to hear. Interventions that draw out students' experiences that truly matter to them will take careful consideration. "What do I want to learn?" taps into the curriculum in second space and seeks to draw the students into making choices that matter to them. Here again, if the two questions are to be connected in an authentic way, the interventions that make that happen will take thoughtful planning. Interventions that bring these two together are created by interaction in third space. Kuhlthau's Six Cs—collaborate, converse, continue, choose, chart, and compose—are intervention strategies intended to create third space, in which the students' world is brought into play for learning the content of the curriculum. "How do I find out?" seeks to draw students into the decision making that drives searching for information for inquiry learning. When third space interaction has been created to bring the students' world and the curriculum together, "What did I learn?" takes on deep personal meaning. "How do I share what I learned?" follows naturally when students have learned something meaningful that they want to share in the community of learners. "What will I do next time?" acknowledges ongoing learning in an inquiry environment, discussed in chapter 8. Interventions that connect the students' world to the curriculum form the essential base for Guided Inquiry.

Intervention for a Community of Learners

Guided Inquiry calls for creating a community of learners in which students learn through social interaction with others. Interventions centering around a community of learners call for a flexible approach to configuring learning groups. Flexible grouping is an important means of intervention in Guided Inquiry. Some interventions are conducted with a whole class, others in small groups or pairs; still others involve guiding individual students. Implementation is based on the instructional team planning the entire scope of the inquiry unit, with strategic interventions as students progress through the stages of the process.

Small groups provide opportunities for students to work jointly with others. The structure of inquiry circles facilitates intervention in small groups. Interventions employing small group interaction enable students to know each other better and to become familiar with each other's work. Over time students gradually form a community of learners who respect and support each other. An important advantage of flexible small groups is the opportunity for students to collaborate with various other students, not necessarily the same group, all the way through the inquiry project. When students know what others are working on, they often give each other ideas on sources of information they have come across that relate to others' areas of inquiry. The instructional team employs small group interaction at the zone of intervention, where having the students think together moves the inquiry process along for each student in the group. Small group intervention can assist students in each of the five types of intervention.

Conversing is the primary activity of small group interaction. Groups made up of five or six provide opportunities for students to have more turns at talking than they would have in a larger group or the whole class. Small groups provide opportunities for students to talk about ideas, to raise further questions, and to get multiple perspectives. Students become comfortable trying out new ideas and taking risks expressing their opinions. Through small group conversation students clarify their ideas and construct knowledge by thinking and reflecting with each other. Intervention strategies of listening, modeling, and encouraging talk, as described in chapter 3, help students engage in meaningful conversations that promote learning. The interactive forum of the community of learners creates an audience for student learning.

Intervention tailored to each stage in the process and the task to be accomplished may indicate a zone of intervention that can best be served by pairs of students working together. Students may be organized in work pairs who have different abilities that enhance each other's inquiry. The most favorable work pairs are organized to the advantage of both of the students. Pairs are most helpful when working together moves the inquiry along for each student.

Small groups and work pairs provide opportunities for students to interact with the instructional team on a more personal level than in the whole class. The instructional team structures the tasks for the small conversation groups or inquiry circles and for the work pairs and closely guides their interaction, stepping in at critical times to provide advice and instruction. Individual conferences with students are scheduled when one-on-one guidance is indicated. Whole class instruction is provided when it is the most efficient intervention for learning about sources, content, process, or learning skills.

In Guided Inquiry the instructional team employs whole class instruction, small group conversations, work pairs, and individual conferences when each is the most effective intervention, enabling the student to do with advice and assistance what he or she cannot do alone or can do only with great difficulty. Inquiry does not need to be an isolated, individual process, although each student must construct her or his own understanding. Collaborative learning in a community of learners enables thinking, construction, and deep understanding. The community of learners fosters the development of research competency and subject knowledge as well as fostering reading comprehension, language development, and social skills.

Planning for Guided Inquiry

Successful inquiry requires careful planning and thoughtful implementation, with insightful interventions at critical points to guide students in their process of learning. As we have discussed, inquiry is a dynamic, creative process, with students' questions driving the inquiry in unexpected directions. Guided Inquiry is not a package that you can apply indiscriminately but rather an approach to learning that is creative for the teacher as well as the students. The intervention strategies in this chapter offer ways to promote learning through inquiry. These interventions can be used as a basis for developing an inquiry program in your school and for planning and implementing an inquiry unit for your students.

The Guided Inquiry team plans together for all stages of the inquiry process and for the assessment of learning. The inquiry unit is developed around a series of session plans to motivate and guide student learning. The term "session" is used rather than "lesson" to emphasize that instruction or teaching a lesson is only one of the interventions to be employed in Guided Inquiry. One way to set up the sessions is to plan each around a starter, a work time, and a reflection. The starter is a whole group meeting in which the students briefly review where they are and decide what needs to be done during the work time. Any formal instruction that is needed on source, content, process, or learning skill is given during the starter. Instruction is developed as a mini-lesson that is applied by students in the work time. In the work time students are organized in work pairs, small groups, or individually, depending on the task to be accomplished and the stage of the inquiry process. Each session closes with a reflection of the whole group on what has been learned and discussion of how to prepare for the next session. Coming together for reflection is an essential part of each session that needs sufficient time to solidify the learning and prepare students for the next stage of work.

The inquiry unit results in an outcome that incorporates an action and a product in which the students display their learning to the other students in the community of learners. The products of inquiry may be as varied as a poster talk, position paper, demonstration, media presentation, or exhibit, to name just a few. The product needs to be suited to the intended audience, which includes the community of learners and any others identified by the group. The product enables the students to learn from each other. Products that are announced at the beginning of the inquiry need to be sufficiently creative and fun to motivate the students to pursue the inquiry. Some of the best products emerge from the inquiry itself, in which students decide how to present their learning as they progress. However, as important as the product is to present and share, it is essential that emphasis be not solely on the product. The product serves as a way to share the learning with others, which is the culminating action of the inquiry process. Without the product the student lacks direction and a sense of completion. However, overemphasis on the product inhibits the experience of the stages of inquiry by closing down the creativity and reflection that fosters learning.

In this chapter we discussed the zone of intervention, where instruction, guidance, and assistance are most effective, and creating third space in a community of learners, where students can draw on their outside-school experience to enhance learning in school. We explored flexible grouping and intervention strategies that foster reflection for deep understanding and basic inquiry abilities for learning from a variety of sources, which can be introduced to young children and developed, reinforced, and applied throughout middle and secondary school. This basic overview of interventions for guiding inquiry offers the foundation for building inquiry learning.

Meeting the Challenge of the 21st-Century School

Over the nine-week information search process, I learned so many things about myself. Previously, I viewed things in black and white and was not willing to compromise. I learned that I was more creative than I previously thought.
—11th-grade student

Guided Inquiry has emerged at a time when people are recognizing that our educational system is not adequately preparing students for the shifting demands of the global information society. The workplace is changing. The way we communicate is changing. Our communities are changing, and there is no reason to believe that things will stand still in the future. Fortunately, educators recognize this, and policy makers agree that schools must be restructured to meet these changes. Guided Inquiry is positioned to bridge any gap between academic success and success in the workplace and in daily living.

Workforce Readiness

The report of the Commission on the Skills of the American Workforce, *Tough Choices for Tough Times* (National Center on Education and the Economy, 2006) reminds us that the shifting economy calls for educated persons: "The best employers the world over will be looking for the most competent, most creative and most innovative people on the face of the earth and will be willing to pay them top dollar for their services. This will be true not just for top professionals and managers, but up and down the length and breadth of the workforce" (p. 7). While routine jobs will continue to be automated and outsourcing a common occurrence, the commission reports that most work will be in the form of "research, development, design, marketing and sales and global supply chain management." In other words, our world will need innovators having "facility with the use of ideas and abstractions needed to manage one's work and drive it through to a successful conclusion, [and the] ability to function well as a member of a team" (p. 14).

Consider how Guided Inquiry addresses these needs. Students become more adept at using ideas and abstractions. They are both encouraged and enabled to synthesize information they find through their own search efforts and share what they've learned through presentations to others.

147

Research is the essence of all inquiry learning and involves locating, evaluating, and using information from a variety of sources. To be effective researchers, however, students must learn how to manage and conduct an extensive inquiry from beginning to end. The ability to manage one's work and see it through to a successful conclusion is a basic requirement of Guided Inquiry. The inquiry process engages students in first identifying questions, then exploring information, and then creating solutions that are both pragmatic and aesthetically pleasing. The guidance element of the program ensures that students are developing competence in reading, writing, and reasoning, essential for success. Teamwork is an essential workplace skill and is a particular hallmark of Guided Inquiry, ensuring that students learn the advantages of working with others as well as the difficulties of accommodating different work styles and perspectives.

Lifelong Learning for Citizenship and Daily Living

A Civic Enterprises study (Bridgeland et al., 2006) reports that 47 percent of students said they quit school because, "it was boring." This "silent epidemic" results in an incredible loss of human talent and potential. Even among students who stay in school and those who move on to higher education, disengagement and lack of motivation diminishes their enthusiasm for deep learning and learning relevant to everyday life. What can be done to solve the serious problem of students who see no relation between their schoolwork and their actual lives?

By drawing on students' lives outside of school, Guided Inquiry captures the teachable moment by matching the inquiry process to the student's stage of development. A perennial dilemma for teachers of preadolescent students in middle school is how to organize learning environments that motivate students academically at a transitional stage of life. By immersing them in highly engaging inquiry projects under the close supervision of an instructional team, such students can develop a sense of expertise and ownership that enables them to see themselves as participants of a larger community.

The early teen years are regarded as an opportune age to prime students for citizenship and daily living. Many schools provide teenage students with opportunities to volunteer in community service projects to meet specific curriculum goals. Guided Inquiry can enrich such experiences by tying research to their community service. What conditions bring about the need for a soup kitchen or food bank? What would make these services more effective in the community? What is needed to create a pocket park in a neighborhood or a help service for the elderly? Participation in a democratic society calls for citizens who can find and use information on emergent issues and then form intelligent opinions that lead to action.

Guided Inquiry also promotes the cross-disciplinary connections needed for innovation and the creation of new ideas, solutions, and perspectives, which in turn foster thoughtfulness and wisdom. Through personal growth, students develop a mindset capable of embracing concepts beyond those they have directly experienced.

A Balanced Approach to Teaching and Learning

Still, some things never change: the need for research-based teaching grounded in the way people learn, information literacy skills, the ability to work as a team, and knowledge of the world in all its forms. We need the benefits Guided Inquiry provides our students. Guided Inquiry is a holistic approach that simultaneously provides five kinds of learning: curriculum content, information literacy, learning strategies, literacy competence, and social skills.

Throughout the 20th century, education was caught in the uncertainty of a pendulum swing from basic skills to process learning. Guided Inquiry offers a balance by providing ways to improve basic skills and knowledge through meaningful inquiry learning. Guided Inquiry gives teachers ways to provide the reflection, reasoning, and practice that students need to become proficient at using basic skills in real situations. It gives teachers ways to enable students to make the transition from learning basic skills to applying and deepening their learning; provides ways for them to enable students to move from learning to read to reading to learn; provides teachers with ways to develop students' writing skills for comprehending and communicating; shows teachers ways to deepen students' understanding of basic science principles, social studies facts, and math concepts; and provides ways to teach information literacy essential for meaningful learning from vast sources of information. In Guided Inquiry teachers find a balance between skills and creativity that develops the higher literacy essential for today and for the future.

Getting Started and Sustaining Change

The end of this book marks a beginning. The processes we describe here probably sound familiar. Perhaps you have teamed with the librarian or teachers in your school, or taught content through an inquiry approach. You may even have used some of these intervention strategies. Your challenge now is to put it all together and take it to a higher level.

Gain Systemic Support

You need to involve the whole school community. As you can imagine, getting the support of your administration is particularly crucial. Although there is an important role for each person in the school community, the success of Guided Inquiry depends on the full support of the head of the school. Without it, success will be spotty at best. Don't let Guided Inquiry be perceived as an anomaly dependent on personality, talent, or compatibility. For Guided Inquiry to take hold, it must be embraced from the top down as well as the bottom up.

So share this text with the administrators, teachers, and librarians in your school and district. Organize brainstorming meetings to come up with a game plan. Plan professional development sessions and workshops to develop the expertise needed for practical application with your students. Organize a community support group that teams school personnel with students, parents, and community leaders. Get buy-in from as many people as possible, to ensure ongoing support over time.

Develop an Implementation Plan

Changing to a Guided Inquiry approach is going to take considerable time and effort. Realize that systemic change requires extensive planning and perseverance. Don't expect results overnight. Realistic expectations and persistence will make it happen. Begin your implementation plan with a description of where you are now, where you would like to be in three years, and the steps you expect to take to get there. Look at your current program. What aspects are already in place? Where are you lacking? Where do you need to rally more support, or get more people on board?

Continual professional development is an essential component that needs to be woven into implementing Guided Inquiry. Don't forget to include it in your implementation plan! Plan workshops that offer team members the knowledge and skills they will need. Do some members need help planning inquiry units? Are they comfortable in team situations? Are they familiar with community resources? Everyone must be on the same page.

Create Networks for Sharing Stories

Guided Inquiry can take many paths, as revealed in the variety of examples included in this book. If nothing else, it requires flexibility of its practitioners, even as it invites the sharing of best practices. As you implement Guided Inquiry, share your story about what works in your school. Describe the interesting and exciting avenues that it has led you and your students to follow. Share successful unit plans and intervention strategies. These stories, as case studies, will help others to work out the problems and possibilities for their students. Use the results of the Student Learning through Inquiry Measure (SLIM) as a basis for discussing student learning and progress. Communicate your findings to other teachers, administrators, and parents. The effect can be powerful.

At the same time, don't forget to benefit from the experiences of others. Share the problems you encounter as well as your successes. Develop discussion networks for sharing how you worked through problems and for soliciting advice on problems you are facing. Online support groups can be organized within your school and school district, or more broadly through state and national organizations and university centers. Such groups can provide excellent opportunities for developing, implementing, and sustaining Guided Inquiry. Share and compare the results of SLIM with other Guided Inquiry teams to identify ways to continue to improve student learning.

School Libraries in 21st-Century Schools

Guided Inquiry is an exciting new form of teaching and learning that has emerged at a critical time for school reform. A new configuration of teaching and learning is called for, one that develops innovative thinkers who can locate, evaluate, and use information wisely for the workplace, citizenship, and daily living. The result is higher levels of information literacy that go beyond fact finding to constructing deep understanding for lifelong learning.

Absolutely central to such reform are new roles for school staff, particularly that of the school librarian. The school library is the logistical center for Guided Inquiry. The team will need a degree of expertise required for designing learning for innovative creativity for the workplace and daily living. Everyone on the team needs to be highly qualified and have a commitment to improving learning. Only you can make it happen, by joining together as a powerful team with the competence and conviction to re-create your school. It is time to move forcefully to meet the demands of the far-reaching structural changes called for in 21st-century learning.

References

American Association of School Librarians (AASL) and Association for Educational Communications and Technology (AECT). (1998). *Information Power: Building Partnerships for Learning*. Chicago: American Library Association.

American Library Association (ALA). (1989). *Presidential Committee on Information Literacy Final Report*. Available at www.ala.org/ala/acrlpubs/whitepapers/presidential.htm.

Bates, M. (1989). "The Design of Browsing and Berry Picking Techniques for Online Search Interface." *Online Review, 13*, 407–424.

Bhabha, H. (1994). *The Location of Culture*. New York: Routledge.

Bridgeland, J., J. Dilulio, and K. Morison. (2006). *The Silent Epidemic: Perspective of Highschool Dropouts*. Available at www.civicenterprises.net/pdfs/thesilentepidemic3-06.pdf.

Bruner, J. (1973). *Beyond the Information Given: Studies in the Psychology of Knowing*. New York: Norton.

———. (1975). *Toward a Theory of Instruction*. Cambridge, MA: Harvard University Press.

———. (1977). *The Process of Education*. Cambridge, MA: Harvard University Press.

———. (1986). *Actual Minds, Possible Worlds*. Cambridge, MA: Harvard University Press.

———. (1990). *Acts of Meaning*. Cambridge, MA: Harvard University Press.

———. (1994). *Inquiry and Reflection*. Albany: State University of New York Press.

Callison, D. (2005). "Enough Already?: Blazing New Trails for School Library Research: Interview with Keith Curry Lance." *School Library Media Research*. Available at www.ala/aaslpubsandjournals/simrb/editorschoiceb/lance/interviewlance.cfm.

Choo, C. (2006). *The Knowing Organization: How Organizations Use Information to Construct Meaning, Create Knowledge, and Make Decisions*. New York: Oxford University Press.

Clay, M. (1990). *An Observation Survey of Literacy Achievement*. Portsmouth, NH: Heinemann.

Daniels, H. (1994). *Literature Circles: Voice and Choice in the Student-centered Classroom*. York, ME: Stenhouse Publishers.

Dewey, J. (1902). *The Child and the Curriculum*. Chicago: Chicago University Press.

———. (1915). *Democracy and Education*. New York: Macmillan.

———. (1933). *How We Think*. Lexington, MA: Heath.

Donham, J., K. Bishop, C. Kuhlthau, and D. Oberg. (2001). *Inquiry Based Learning: Lessons from Library Power*. Worthington, OH: Linworth.

Elkind, D. (1976). *Child Development and Education: A Piagetian Perspective*. London: Oxford University Press.

Ellis, D. (1989). "A Behavioral Approach to Information Retrieval System Design." *Journal of Documentation, 45,* 171–212.

———. (1992). "The Physical and Cognitive Paradigms in Information Retrieval Research." *Journal of Documentation, 48,* 45–64.

Emig, J. (1971). *The Composing Process of Twelfth Graders.* Urbana, IL: National Council of Teachers of English.

Friedman, T. (2006). "Creativity and the Global Employee." NYTimes.com, December 15.

Gallas, K. (1995). *Talking Their Way into Science: Hearing Children's Questions and Theories, Responding with Curricula.* New York: Teachers College Press.

Gardner, H. (1983). *Frames of Mind: The Theory of Multiple Intelligences.* New York: Basic Books.

Gaver, M. (1963). *Effectiveness of Centralized Library Service in Elementary Schools.* 2nd ed. New Brunswick, NJ: Rutgers University Press.

Gee, J. (1992). *The Social Mind: Language, Ideology, and Social Practice.* New York: Bergin & Garvey.

———. (2000). "New Literacy Studies: From the 'Socially Situated' to the Work of the Social." In *Situated Literacies: Reading Writing in Context,* edited by D. Barton, M. Hamilton, and R. Ivanic. London: Routledge.

Gross, M. (1998). "The Imposed Query: Implications for Library Service Evaluation." *Reference and User Services Quarterly, 37,* 290–299.

Gutierrez, K., B. Rymes, and J. Larson. (1995). "Script, Counterscript and Underlife in the Classroom: James Brown versus *Brown v. the Board of Education.*" *Harvard Educational Review, 65,* 3, 445–471.

Harada, V., and J. Yoshina. (2004). *Inquiry Learning through Librarian-teacher Partnerships.* Worthington, OH: Linworth Publishing.

———. (2005). *Assessing Learning: Librarians and Teachers as Partners.* Westport, CT: Libraries Unlimited/Greenwood Press.

Harste, J. (1994). "Literacy as Curricular Conversations about Knowledge, Inquiry, and Morality." In *Theoretical Models and Processes of Reading.* 4th ed. Edited by R. B. Ruddell, M. R. Ruddell, and H. Singer. Newark, DE: International Reading Association: 1220–1242.

Hartzell, G. (1997, November). "The Invisible School Librarian: Why Other Educators Are Blind to Your Value." *School Library Journal.* Available at www.schoollibraryjournal.com/article/CA152978.htm.

———. (2002). *Capitalizing on the School Library's Potential to Positively Affect Student Achievement.* White House Conference on School Libraries. Available: www.imls.gov/pubs/ whitehouse0602/garyhartzell.htm.

Heath, S. (1998). "Working through Language." In *Kids Talk: Strategic Language Use in Later Childhood,* edited by S. Hoyle and C. Adger. New York: Oxford University Press.

Heath, S., E. Boehncke, and S. Wolf. (2005). *Made for Each Other: Creative Sciences and Arts in the Secondary School.* London: Creative Partnerships.

Hopkins, D. , and D. Zweizeg, guest eds. (1999). "Library Power Program Evaluation—Theme Issue." *School Libraries Worldwide, 5.*

Keene, E., and S. Zimmerman. (1997). *Mosaic of Thought: Teaching Comprehension in a Reader's Workshop.* Portsmouth, NH: Heinemann.

Keirsey, D., and M. Bates. (1978). *Please Understand Me: Character and Temperament Types.* Del Mar, CA: Prometheus Nemesis Books.

Kelly, G. (1963). *A Theory of Personality: The Psychology of Personal Constructs.* New York: Norton.

Kozol, J. (2005). *The Shame of the Nation: The Restoration of Apartheid Schooling in America.* New York: Random House.

Kuhlthau, C. (1981). *School Librarians' Grade-by Grade Activities Program: A Complete Sequential Skills Plan for Grades K–8.* Nyack, NY: The Center for Applied Research in Education/Prentice Hall.

———. (1985a). *Teaching the Library Research Process.* New York: The Center for Applied Research in Education. (2nd ed., Scarecrow Press, 1994.)

———. (1985b). "A Process Approach to Library Skills Instruction." *School Library Media Quarterly, 13,* 1, 35–40.

———. (1987a). "An Emerging Theory of Library Instruction." *School Library Media Quarterly, 16,* 1, 23–28.

———. (1987b). "Cognitive Development and Student's Research." *School Library Journal, 11,* 46.

———. (1988a). "Perceptions of the Information Search Process in Libraries: A Study of Changes from High School Through College." *Information Processing and Management, 24,* 4, 419–427.

———. (1988b). "Longitudinal Case Studies of the Information Search Process of Users in Libraries." *Library and Information Science Research, 10,* 3, 257–304.

———. (1988c). "Meeting the Information Needs of Children and Young Adults: Basing Library Media Programs on Developmental States." *Journal of Youth Services in Libraries, 2,* 1, 51–57.

———. (1988d). "Developing a Model of the Library Search Process: Investigation of Cognitive and Affective Aspects." *Reference Quarterly, 28,* 2, 232–242.

———. (1989a). "The Information Search Process of High-, Middle-, and Low-Achieving High School Seniors." *School Library Media Quarterly, 17,* 4, 224–228.

———. (1989b). "Information Search Process: A Summary of Research and Implications for School Library Media Programs." *School Library Media Quarterly, 18,* 5, 19–25.

———. (1990a). "The Information Search Process: From Theory to Practice." *Journal of Education for Library and Information Science Continuing Education, 31,* 1.

———; with B. Turock, M. George, and R. Belvin. (1990b). "Validating a Model of the Search Process: A Comparison of Academic, Public, and School Library Users." *Library and Information Science Research, 12,* 1, 5–32.

———. (1991). "Inside the Search Process: Information Seeking from the User's Perspective." *Journal of the American Society for Information Science (JASIS), 42,* 5, 361–371.

———. (1993a). "Implementing a Process Approach to Information Skills: A Study Identifying Indicators of Success in Library Media Programs." *School Library Media Quarterly, 22,* 1, 11–18.

———. (1993b). "A Principle of Uncertainty for Information Seeking." *Journal of Documentation, 49,* 4, 339–355.

———. (1994a). "Assessing the Library Research Process." In *Assessment and the School Library Media Center,* edited by C. Kuhlthau, with associate eds. E Goodin and M. McNally. Englewood, CO: Libraries Unlimited.

———. (1994b). "Impact of the Information Search Process Model on Library Services." *Reference Quarterly RQ, 34,* 1, 21–26.

———. (1994c). "Students and the Information Search Process: Zones of Intervention for Librarians." In *Advances in Librarianship,* edited by I. Godden. New York: Academic Press: 57–72.

———. (1995). "The Process of Learning from Information." *School Libraries Worldwide 1,* 1, 1–12.

———. (1996). *Seeking Meaning: A Process Approach to Library and Information Services.* Norwood, NJ: Ablex.

———. (1997). "Learning in Digital Libraries: An Information Search Process Approach." *Library Trends, 45,* 4, 708–724.

———. (1999a). "Opportunities for Student Learning in Library Power Schools." *School Libraries Worldwide, 5,* 2, 80–96.

———. (1999b). "Accommodating the User's Information Search Process: Challenges for Information Retrieval System Designers." *Bulletin of the American Society for Information Science 50th Anniversary Special Issue on Information Seeking and Finding, 25,* 3, 12–16.

———. (1999c). "The Role of Experience in the Information Search Process of an Early Career Information Worker: Perceptions of Uncertainty, Complexity, Construction and Sources." *Journal of the American Society for Information Science (JASIS), 50,* 5, 399–412.

———. (1999d). "Opportunities for Student Learning in Library Power Schools." *School Libraries Worldwide, 5,* 2, 80–96.

———. (1999e). "Information Seeking in Context." *Information Processing and Management, 35,* 6, theme issue.

———. (2001a). "Information Search Process of Lawyers: A Call for 'Just for Me' Information Services." *Journal of Documentation, 57,* 1, 25–43.

———, with M. McNally. (2001b). "Information Seeking for Learning: A Study of Librarians' Perceptions of Learning in School Libraries, *The New Review of Information Behaviour Research, 2,* 167–177.

———. (2004). *Seeking Meaning: A Process Approach to Library and Information Services.* 2nd ed. Westport, CT: Libraries Unlimited.

Lance, K., et al. (2001). *Proof of the Power: Recent Research on the Impact of School Library Media Programs on the Academic Achievement of U.S. Public School Students.* Syracuse, NY: ERIC Clearing House on Information and Technology. ED 1.310/ 2:456861.

Limberg, L. (1997). "Information Use for Learning Purposes." In *Information Seeking in Context: Proceedings of an International Conference on Research in Information Needs, Seeking and Use in Different Contexts*, edited by P. Vakkari, R. Savolainen, and B. Dervin. London: Taylor Graham: 275–289.

Limberg, L., and M. Alexandersson. (2003). "The School Library as a Space for Learning." *School Libraries Worldwide, 9,* 1, 1–15.

Loertscher, D., and R. Todd. (2003). *We Boost Achievement: Evidence Based Practice for School Library Media Specialists.* Salt Lake City, UT: Hi Willow Research and Publishing.

Maniotes, L. (2005). "The Transformative Power of Literary Third Space." Ph.D. dissertation, School of Education, University of Colorado, Boulder.

Maybin, J. (1999). Framing and Evaluation in Ten- to Twelve-year-old School Children's Use of Repeated, Appropriated, and Reported Speech in Relation to Their Induction into Educational Procedures and Practices. *Text, 19,* 4, 459–484.

McNally, M. (2005). "Analysis of Students' Mental Models: Using the Internet in an Authentic Learning Situation." Ph.D. dissertation, Graduate School, Rutgers, The State University of New Jersey.

Mehan, H. (1979). *Learning Lessons.* Cambridge, MA: Harvard University Press.

Mercer, N. (2000). *Words and Minds: How We Use Language to Think Together.* London: Rutledge.

Moje, E., K. Ciechanowski, and R. Athan. (2001). "Looking for Third Space: Exploring Intersections of Community and Classroom Discourse." Paper presented at the Annual Meeting of the National Reading Conference, San Antonio, TX, December.

Moje, E., K. Ciechanowski, K. Kramer, L. Ellis, R. Carrillo, and T. Collazo. (2004). "Working Toward Third Space in Content-area Literacy: An Examination of Everyday Funds of Knowledge and Discourse. *Reading Research Quarterly, 39,* 1, 38–70.

Moll, L., and J. Greenberg. (1990). "Creating Zones of Possibilities: Combining Social Contexts for Instruction." In *Vygotsky and Education: Instructional Implications and Applications of Sociohistorical Psychology,* edited by L.C. Moll. Cambridge, UK: Cambridge University Press: 319–348.

National Center on Education and the Economy. (2006). *Tough Choices for Tough Times: The Report of the New Commission on the Skills of the American Workforce.* Available: www.skillscommission.org.

National Council for the Social Studies. (1989). *Expectations of Excellence: Curriculum Standards for Social Studies.* Silver Spring, MD: National Council of Teachers of English.

National Council of Teachers of English. (1996). *Standards for the English Language Arts.* Newark, DE: IRA; Urbana, IL: NCTE.

Oatman, E. (2006). "Overwhelming Evidence: Libraries Make a Big Difference in Students' Lives." *School Library Journal,* January, 56–59.

O'Connor, M., and S. Michaels. (1996). "Shifting Participant Frameworks: Orchestrating Thinking Practices in Group Discussion." In *Discourse, Learning and Schooling,* edited by D. Hicks. Cambridge, UK: University of Cambridge Press: 63–103.

Ogle, D. S. (1986). "K-W-L Group Instructional Strategy." In *Teaching Reading as Thinking,* edited by A. Palincsar, D. Ogle, B. Jones, and E. Carr. Teleconference Resource Guide. Alexandria, VA: Association for Supervision and Curriculum Development: 11–17.

Oppenheimer, T. (2003). *The Flickering Mind: Saving Education from the False Promise of Technology.* New York: Random House.

Public Information Resources, Inc. (2002). *Diverse Brains: Using Brain Research to Enrich the Classroom: Proceedings of the Seventh Conference on Learning and the Brain.* Boston: Public Information Resources.

———. (2006). *Optimizing the Brain and Body to Improve Learning: Proceedings of the Fifteenth Conference on Learning and the Brain.* Boston: Public Information Resources.

Rice, R., M. McCreadie, and S. Chang. (2001). *Accessing and Browsing Information and Communication.* Cambridge: Massachusetts Institute of Technology Press.

Taylor, D., and C. Dorsey-Gaines. (1988). *Growing up Literate: Learning from Inner-city Families.* Portsmouth, NH: Heinemann.

Todd, R. (1995). "Integrated Information Skills Instruction: Does It Make a Difference?" *School Library Media Quarterly, 23*, 2, 133–139.

Todd, R., and C. Kuhlthau. (2005a). "Student Learning through Ohio School Libraries, Part 1: How Effective School Libraries Help Students." *School Libraries Worldwide, 11*, 1, 89–110.

———. (2005b). "Student Learning through Ohio School Libraries, Part 2: Faculty Perceptions of Effective School Libraries." *School Libraries Worldwide, 11*, 1, 89–110.

Todd, R., C. Kuhlthau, and J. Heinstrom. (2005) *Impact of School Libraries on Student Learning.* Institute of Museum and Library Services Leadership Grant Project Report. Available: http://cissl.scils.rutgers.edu/research/imls.

Tomlinson, C. (1999). *The Differentiated Classroom: Responding to the Needs of All Learners.* Alexandria, VA: Association for Supervision and Curriculum Development.

Vygotsky, L. (1978). *Mind in Society: The Development of Higher Psychological Processes.* Edited nad translated by M. Cole, V. John-Steiner, S. Scribner, and E. Soubermen. Cambridge, MA: Harvard University Press. (Original work published 1934.)

Wells, G. (2000). "Dialogic Inquiry in Education: Building on the Legacy of Vygotsky." In *Vygotskian Perspectives on literacy Research: Constructing Meaning through Collaborative Inquiry,* edited by C. D. Lee and P. Smagorinsky. Cambridge, UK: Cambridge University Press: 51–85).

Whelan, D. (2006). "2006 SLJ/Thomson Gale Giant Step Awards School Library Winner–Research High." *School Library Journal,* May, 47–49.

Wiggins, G. , and J. McTighe. (1998). *Understanding by Design.* Alexandria, VA: Association for Supervision and Curriculum Development.

Williams, D., and C. Wavell. (2006). "Untangling Spaghetti? The Complexity of Developing Information Literacy in Secondary School Students." In *Final Report on Research Funded by Society for Educational Studies.* Aberdeen: The Robert Gordon University.

Literature Cited

Blume, J. (2003). *Superfudge.* New York: Puffin.

Curtis C. P. (1999). *Bud, Not Buddy.* New York: Delacorte Press.

DiCamillo, K. (2000). *Because of Winn-Dixie.* Cambridge, MA: Candlewick Press.

Fitzgerald, F. Scott (1925). *The Great Gatsby.* New York: Scribner's.

Halse Anderson, L. (2000). *Fever 1793.* New York: Scholastic.

Lewis, C. S. (1978). *The Lion, the Witch, and the Wardrobe.* New York: HarperTrophy.

Index

About the Authors

Carol Collier Kuhlthau is Professor Emerita of Library and Information Science at Rutgers University, where she directed the graduate program in school librarianship that has been rated number one in the country by *U.S. News & World Report*. She achieved the rank of Professor II, a special rank at Rutgers requiring additional review beyond that for full professor. She also chaired the Department of Library and Information Science and was the founding director of the Center for International Scholarship in School Libraries (CISSL). She is internationally known for her groundbreaking research on the information search process and for the ISP model of affective, cognitive, and physical aspects in six stages of information seeking and use. She has authored *Seeking Meaning: A Process Approach to Library and Information Services* (2004) and *Teaching the Library Research Process* (2004) and published widely in refereed journals and edited volumes. She has received numerous awards and held visiting appointments at universities around the world.

Leslie Kuhlthau Maniotes is a National Board Certified Teacher who recently completed a Ph.D. in instructional curriculum in content areas at the University of Colorado, Boulder. She is a K–12 literacy specialist with Reading Recovery Certification and a M.Ed. in reading. With 11 years of classroom experience, she has led workshops and teacher advancement training and taught undergraduate and graduate courses in the School of Education at the University of Colorado.

Ann Kuhlthau Caspari is a specialist in museum education with a master's degree in teaching from George Washington University. She has extensive background as a museum educator at the National Building Museum, Calvert Marine Museum in Maryland, Paul Revere House, and Newport Historical Society. Currently she is the Senior Museum Educator for the Smithsonian Early Enrichment Center, where she frequently conducts workshops for teachers on the use of museum objects to enhance the curriculum.

Guided Inquiry

CPSIA information can be obtained at www.ICGtesting.com
Printed in the USA
LVOW051304110112

263361LV00004B/43/P